THROUGH ISAAC'S EYES

ᐒHROUGH ISAAC'S EYES

CROSSING OF CULTURES,

COMING OF AGE,

AND THE BOND

BETWEEN

FATHER AND SON

DANIEL BARTH PETERS

ZondervanPublishingHouse
Grand Rapids, Michigan

A Division of HarperCollinsPublishers

Through Isaac's Eyes
Copyright © 1996 by Daniel Barth Peters

Requests for information should be addressed to:

ZondervanPublishingHouse
Grand Rapids, Michigan 49530

Library of Congress Cataloging-in-Publication Data

Peters, Daniel Barth, 1954–.
    Through Isaac's eyes / Daniel Barth Peters.
        p. cm.
    ISBN 0-310-20376-7 (softcover)
    1. Peters, Daniel Barth, 1954– . 2. Children of missionaries—United
States—Biography. 3. Vietnamese Conflict, 1961–1975—Personal narratives,
American. 4. Peters, John W. I. Title.
BV2094.5.P48 1996
266'.0092-dc20   95-20912
                                                                         CIP

Edited by Lyn Cryderman and Gerard Terpstra
Interior design by Sue Koppenol
Vietnamese translation and calligraphy by Vinh Nguyen, Trung Pham,
    Tuan Ho, and Binh Tran

Printed in the United States of America

96 97 98 99 00 01 02 / ❖ DH/ 10 9 8 7 6 5 4 3 2 1

To Lynda

CONTENTS

Acknowledgments

Without a listener the story remains untold. A circle of friends, standing palms toward the fire, stood by and listened as I began to retell this story. Susan Alexander, Virgle Hedgcoth, Kate Kogut Berneking, Dean Blevins, JoAnn Blevins, Ellen Bossen, Loran Mark Bossen, Millie Byers, Tim Byers, Ben Cooley, Dianne Cooley, Kathryn Diaz, Michael Diaz, Ed Ezaki, Gretchen Ezaki, LeeAnn Meyer, Charles Mitchell, Jamie Musson, Rod Musson, Brenth Smith and Lori Smith have supported, nurtured, financed, encouraged, questioned and challenged me during the writing of this book. They have each, by listening in their own way, helped me to see through Isaac's eyes.

Many professors and mentors have guided my life and shaped my storytelling. However, Mariel Hampton, Robert Matson, Phil Rohler, Cole Dawson Lou Foltz, Thomas Pappas, Allan Axelrad, Wayne Hobson, Karen Lystra, Michael Steiner, Lori Dick, Jennifer Fog-Toops, Irene Loewen, Donald N. Larson, Robert Dawidoff and Ann Taves each contributed to the long development of this particular story through conversations, teachings, readings, suggestions and critical reviews as well as insightful, and sometimes uncanny, counsel and commentary.

Ron Haynes, my agent, and Lyn Cryderman, my editor, had a vision for the book, and both worked hard to see that it was published. Special thanks to Alma Peoples, J. T. Peoples, Bill Dennis and Carol Dennis.

Family on both sides of the aisle have read the story, although not all have been able to face it. Carolyn and Rich Hagenbaugh, Carmen and Roger Wiens, Conrad and Mar-Jean Peters and John and Helen Wood have supported and embraced me always.

The gentle grace of Lynda Dianne Wood Peters nurtured this book from beginning to end. She was there on that long stretch of Texas highway when the story of the beggar woman crystallized and I understood for the first time a piece of my own life. Her presence with me through the recounting of each story, and sometimes for days after, provided the sustenance I needed to finish. Words smoke away, cindered by the burden of being unable to say it well enough—thank you.

Daddy is gone, and Mother doesn't recognize me anymore, and while they would have rather had a commentary on the book of Romans, I hope they would have found some of God's grace herein as well.

Finally, a special thanks to the hundreds of missionary kids whom I have met, known, read and worked with—whose stories have not yet been heard. Each story is different, but every memory is valid.

In this book I am true to my own memory. To protect the privacy of those remembered, I have changed the names of certain people and locales. While I have benefited from the support of many, any errors are solely mine.

21And it came to pass after these things that God did tempt Abraham, and said unto him, Abraham: and he said, Behold, here I am.

And he said, Take now thy son, thine only son Isaac, whom thou lovest, and get thee into the land of Moriah; and offer him there for a burnt offering upon one of the mountains which I will tell thee of.

And Abraham rose up early in the morning, and saddled his ass, and took two of his young men with him, and Isaac his son, and clave the wood for the burnt offering, and rose up, and went unto the place of which God had told him.

Then on the third day Abraham lifted up his eyes, and saw the place afar off.

And Abraham said unto his young men, Abide ye here with the ass; and I the lad will go yonder and worship, and come again to you.

And Abraham took the wood of the burnt offering, and laid it upon Isaac his son, and he took the fire in his hand, and a knife; and they went both of them together.

And Isaac spoke unto Abraham, his father, and said, My father: and he said, Behold the fire and the wood: but where is the lamb for a burnt offering?

And Abraham said, My son, God will provide himself a lamb for a burnt offering; so they went both of them together.

And they came to the place which God had told him of; and Abraham built an altar there, and laid the wood in order, and bound Isaac, his son, and laid him on the altar upon the wood.

And Abraham stretched forth his hand, and took the knife to slay his son.

And the angel of the LORD called unto him out of heaven, and said, Abraham, Abraham: and he said, Here am I.

And he said, Lay not thine hand upon the lad, neither do thou anything unto him; for now I know that thou fearest God, seeing thou hast not withheld thy son, thine only son from me.

And Abraham lifted his eyes, and looked, and behold, behind him a ram caught in a thicket by his horns: and Abraham went and took the ram, and offered up for a burnt offering in the stead of his son.

And Abraham called the name of that place Jehovah-jireh, as it is said to this day, In the mount of the LORD it shall be seen.

GENESIS 22:1–14, KING JAMES VERSION

Introduction

My memories of Vietnam reside in me like Kodak snapshots pasted in an old scrapbook. They have not faded with time. They are still stark in focus, still intense in resolution. Even so, it took time, writing a little at a time, to live again within them—to see Phu's plastic sandal, to smell the gunpowder, to touch the grass, to feel the breeze from the fan circling overhead, to taste the water in my lunch pail, to be so alone that I cannot move from its weight. These snapshots hold green palm trees, black lacquered vases, red dirt, coral sunsets, teal oceans, and a color I never identified, that color of the river that seemed to never move through the heart of Saigon. Perhaps it was the color of war—oil and gas and waste and blood and garbage and disease and death. One of Daddy's greatest fears was that I would fall in and be swallowed up. They might fish me out before drowning, but not before millions of invisible organisms had begun devouring my flesh and I would be lost to it—and to him.

The spaces in my scrapbook, in between the photos, are the color of the Saigon River. I don't know what happened to those spaces in my memory, those people, those events that moved me through time, but they are no longer here. There is more empty space in the book now than there once was, and Vietnam occupies a less painful space in me. To those whom I have cut out of my memory—each person, each neighborhood, each kindness, each smile, each scream—I am sorry. To keep my self I could not keep all of you. Perhaps if I searched

11

I might find a few more snapshots, but herein lies what remains, not as ashes but as the sinews of my life.

This is a book of remembered stories. Stories of a thirteen-year-old boy and the middle-aged preacher who took him on a journey. A journey of coming of age while crossing cultures. Perhaps if Daddy was anything, he was a storyteller. As a pastor he preached "the old, old story," and as a missionary he traveled because he had "a story to tell to the nations." Barbara Myerhoff wrote in *Number Our Days* (Touchstone Books, 1980) that we are "homo narrans"—people of the story. These are the stories that make me human. I am only as human as my memory.

San Bruno

1967

Cái Thùng

1

The Barrel

San Bruno, California

When I went down the stairs and turned right into the garage, it was standing by the back window—the brown cardboard barrel with the yellow printing on the side from Thompson Styrofoam Company in South City. Conrad and my cousin Ken worked summer jobs at Thompson Styrofoam and got these cardboard barrels with metal tops for us. The barrel once held billions of tiny foam balls that were to be heat-smushed into coffee cups. Now it was to contain my life.

Daddy was taking a break and stood resting part of his weight on the barrel, one leg crossed in front of the other. He had been packing all morning, and I could tell he was weary. His achey back was achey and his arms and feet were tired. He was wearing, for Daddy anyway, old clothes—a pair of black pants, shiny from too many travels under Mother's iron and a cream-colored shirt open at the neck, with the sleeves rumpled up two full cuff lengths. On his feet were a pair of those hated hard nylon dress socks and scuffed but firmly tied brown shoes. He had been waiting for me, resting, since calling my name up the stairs a few minutes ago. We were moving from San Bruno, California, to Saigon, South Vietnam, and the time had come to put my stuff in the barrel.

On the concrete floor in front of the barrel was piled a huge stack of toys, mitts, balls, pictures, games, school projects, and the rest of the stuff that had been extracted from my closet and from under my bed and from anyplace else around the house that enveloped my life. The plaque from school, the mitt I found at the church picnic two summers ago, my shoe box of baseball cards, some old valentines from my cousins in St. Louis. All the meanderings of my entire life could pretty much be retraced by these articles and their place in the house. Things in boxes in the basement were old hat, selected by Mother for saving; they included stupid things like a lock of hair from my first birthday's haircut. Things under my bed were largely forgotten but not totally irrelevant. Things in the bottom of my half of the closet were pretty current, and that, of course, is why I kept them there—for fast retrieval. The redwood box on top of my dresser, the box with the photo of the drive-through tree pasted on the top and the words "Mt. Hermon Christian Conference Ground" burnt across the corner, held secret things. Those secrets included notes passed in church, the names of my favorite girlfriends (in descending order), and my always-slim supply of Juicy Fruit gum.

With the exception of my clothes heading for the Orient (which Mother was in charge of, having written ahead to missionaries living there to see what clothes were appropriate for both the weather and for Christians in Vietnam) my entire life mounded in the center of the garage floor. A family from Cedar Avenue Baptist Church bought the house and offered to let us store some stuff in the basement. My allotment of space was big enough for my all-chrome stingray bike with its black banana seat and one cardboard barrel.

Daddy had made a radical commitment to go to the mission field. At 53 he was quitting the ministry and selling the house, car and furniture. He was breaking up the family and going onward to war, a Christian soldier. At this moment the Epiphany of his commitment was playing a more hollow note as it swirled downward and echoed up at me from the bottom of the barrel.

For the rest of the afternoon, Daddy standing beside me, I picked up one toy after the other and had to make that decision. Would it go into the barrel or into the trash? I picked up an old yellow dog, stuffed with gray cotton that was herniating out of the seam in the stomach. It had not been particularly important to me for several years now. I had even taken it under the house and peed on its head once. But this was a dog given to me by Aunt Sally at Baden Baptist Church, when we left there to come to San Bruno. I did not remember much about actually getting it, but that dog told me I came from somewhere before coming here. That was not good enough; I would no longer be from here soon, so why should I care about where I came from before here? I threw the yellow dog off to one side. It landed with a dull thump on the floor and skidded sideways toward the furnace, where it stopped dead.

I picked up a box of old records. They were mostly rejects from Carolyn and Carmen, scratched 45s that they had outgrown or outworn. I used to go into my closet, clear off a place on the floor, put down a blanket and a pillow, and listen to them in the dark, leaving the door open just a crack to let in enough light to change the record, "Clang, clang, clang, went the trolley." Clang, crack, crash went the records. My shoe box of baseball cards—mostly a motley collection but including my prized trio of Mays, McCovey, and Marichal, along with Gaylord Perry—started a new pile. This pile I would give away to my friends either on Pinecrest Drive or at Cedar Avenue Baptist. Creating this pile made things a little easier; at least I did not have to throw away all the stuff I wasn't keeping. Into the barrel went my mitts and baseballs and bats. That was automatic. In went some awards and papers with A plus written right across the top.

"Hey, let me see that one, Pal," Daddy said. "Boy, that is great work."

I mumbled what all kids mumble in response to parental praise for school work, that mixture of hot embarrassment and cool pride.

Some things were harder than others to decide. I would linger, looking at a crack in red plastic, feeling the stitches on the globe. I thought, *I have had this yellow dump truck since kindergarten*, and remembered the great roads and valleys and hills that it made in the dirt in my backyard—black dirt, moist from fog above yet warm from hell below, dirt sticking to the tires and getting in the hinges and scratching the plastic windows, dirt defining the ridges of my fingernails. I picked up a peel of gray bark that I had pulled off one of the eucalyptus trees at the top of the hill and could never bring myself to throw away due to its odd shape, bluish color, and rumpled texture. It seemed to capture the spirit of that stand of trees. There were forts, Man From U.N.C.L.E. strategies, animals, fights, and fungi in those trees. What should I do? How important was this to me? What was my life that should go into the barrel and what was not me that could be thrown away? What pieces of me would end up in the trash, and what pieces in the barrel, and what pieces would I give away to my friends?

Daddy pulled up a folding chair and sat. This was taking a while, and time was something we did not have much of. There was packing, passports, partings and other Peters' things to do. He wanted me to hurry just a little, but he could not bring himself to say it. I could tell, though. Daddy was always able to radiate his sense of things and to gently direct me without words. But he knew this was painful for me and was trying to give me some space. I could see it in his face. His pain was for me, and I could feel his pain for me more than my own. This was not the first time that I had felt Daddy's pain for me.

One Sunday morning last spring found us Cedar Avenue Baptist boys restless. We played tag among the cars between

Sunday school and church, with Mr. Holmes' Borg Warner serving as home base. Church had already started when we slithered in and sat sweating together in the back. We were usually pirated away by one parent or another and split up into less volatile numbers for church. But this Sunday we were sitting eight across, nearly one whole row's worth.

The service went well enough during the singing, announcements and offering. During the preaching, though, Dennis decided one of us had taken his pen, so he could not write notes. There was much discussion about who had the pen, accompanied by general snickering and heads bobbing back and forth. Eventually, Dennis decided that I had it in my inside suit coat pocket, and before I knew what was happening he was out of his chair and digging through my pockets. Amid my protests we were lost in this near epic struggle when I heard Daddy's preaching voice stop and then cut right through to the quick of my soul. "Danny, please go and sit by your Mother," his voice boomed. The church was dead quiet; I was just plain dead. Dennis froze, and every kid in that row suddenly converted to sainthood. I willed my jellied knees to stand up, stand up in that quiet, in that stillness, and pushed my way through the humid air tangled with vines of emotion down the entire length of the church, every eye eyeing, to sit by Mother in the second row. Getting "called down" from the pulpit was worse than going to the dentist. There was little on this earth that was worse. It was discipline through public humiliation. In my case from both the Prophet of God and Daddy.

Avoiding Daddy after the service, I rode home with Mother and was in my bedroom taking off my suit when he came in. Trembling, I thought I was going to get spanked for misbehaving in church. Instead, he kneeled down in front of me, and with a tear-filled voice he apologized for picking me out of boys' row. "I'm sorry, Pal," he said. "I should not have called you down in front of the whole church. I shouldn't have singled you out." I immediately threw my arms around him and sobbed, my heart broken that there had been distance between us and for the stern rebuke I had seen in his eyes. I choked out the story that Dennis would not leave me alone and I could not make him stop. He did not take his arms from around me until we were done and then we went in to eat. It was through times like these that I had learned to trust Daddy and to recognize his love for me.

We were now packing this barrel because God had called and we had answered. God would be faithful. Caught between the pain of seeing me throw my toys away and the knowing that down deep this world was not our home was a tender pain for Daddy, a pain perhaps unfamiliar to those not so deeply committed. To be in the world, but not of it, was the most bittersweet knowledge that a boy my age could have. I had heard of it and even sung it—

> *This world is not my home,*
> *I'm just a-passing through.*
> *If Heaven's not my home,*
> *Then, Lord, what will I do?*

But until this moment that song had been just a Sunday school chorus that we sang, with my grandmother, Momoo, putting a little gospel thump on the piano. Now, however, I realized we believed those words. We acted on those words. They were for us, here and now. If this world was not our home, then certainly 2130 Pinecrest Drive was not either.

When I got done, Daddy helped me pack some newspapers around the top of the things, although the bat handles kept poking out. We put the metal lid on, fastened a big ring around it, snapped it into place, and closed a padlock through the loop. He took out his big felt-tip pen and wrote on the side, "Danny's Things—August 1967." We rolled the barrel over to the side of the garage with the rest of our stuff. As I headed up the stairs to my emptied room, I turned the corner of the stairs and looked back. Daddy checked his to-do list and scratched off "Danny's barrel."

All that had been mine—Conrad's and my room, the top bunk overlooking San Francisco International Airport, the stuff in the bottom of the closet and under the bed—was either gone or in a barrel in the basement of a house that was no longer ours. The things that had brought me such happiness, defined my status in the neighborhood, were now as irrelevant as Daddy always believed they should have been. I did not know then that I would never again be able to sort out the piles of my life, throw some away, stuff the rest in a barrel and snap on the lid.

2
Jet Plane

San Bruno

One day in September, just after Labor Day, we were all hanging around San Francisco airport waiting to go to Vietnam. Carolyn and Rich, Carmen and Roger, and Conrad along with Momoo and Aunt Esther's family were all there. More than that, there was the Cedar Avenue gang. Michelle was there too. She came to say good-bye, bringing those lanky summer-browned legs, which made her taller than I, sungoldened hair of brown, and eyes full of wonder. I wanted her to be mine and to take her with me. The closest we came to saying good-bye was when in the confusion and the crowds and the hugs I turned to wave before I walked down the ramp and turned left, toward Vietnam.

All of our official good-byes had already been said. There had been a ritualistically embarrassing Sunday night service in traditional Baptist style, a bit formal and a bit crude, with a sniffle for good grieving measure. The next day there was the all-church Labor Day picnic. One last day to eat hot dogs, play softball, race in gunny sacks, and stain my knees with American grass moist from fog above and earthworms below. One last day to slap Harley on the back for batting me in from third. This was the parting, this was the tearing away of a pastor from his flock. Blest be the tie that binds. Blest be the fabric as it rends. Not believing in unnecessary grief, prolonged pain, or public foibles, Mother and Daddy had set up an escape plan so that there would be no good-byes, no tears. Conrad would bring the car around at a set time. Then Daddy would give the signal and we would jump up, shout, "Bye!" hop into the car, and roar off to the mission field. Good-byes were for people who really wanted to stay. We had our eyes set on things above and would not be held back. There was no grief, only joy, in serving the Most High.

When the small group of insiders showed up to say good-bye at the airport, it was all done. We were already gone. If we had not yet made peace with it, there was a truce in the air. I was going on an adventure halfway around the world. Mother had calm purposefulness about her. Daddy was enlarged from his duty and dreams coalescing into a lived moment.

Once on the plane, Daddy suggested we time the take-off from the first roar of the jets to the moment of buoyancy. It was 38 seconds. Having the window seat, I sat sideways, plastered to the window. The plane banked toward the Pacific as we climbed over San Bruno Mountain. There in the distance was our ridge, with the narrow stand of eucalyptus cutting the neighborhood off from the fields beyond. Somewhere down there Todd and the Pinecrest gang were playing "Man from U.N.C.L.E.," crashing through the underbrush, Todd as Napoleon Solo calling for Ilya Kuryakin to follow. Ilya now played by somebody else. The view became partially blocked by the under-hangings of a few clouds. When they passed from view, the coastline was straight down, Devils Slide foaming at the mouth waiting to swallow more victims. The excitement of Hawaii was just hours ahead. This was a life I deserved. It would be just like me to be the one to go to the Orient. To the wars and to the jungles. Danny Orlis, Christian boy detective, had done it in dozens of Christian novels I had read. So would I. I was a soldier in the Lord's Army. We had sung that song many times in Sunday school, a chance to let off childhood energy with the accompanying motions of swooping planes and machine gun fire . . . .

I'm in the Lord's Army.
I'm in the Lord's Army.
Marching in the infantry,
Riding in the cavalry,
Shooting the artillery.
I'm in the Lord's Army.

After Hawaii we had a long ride to Tokyo. It was on this ride that I first felt the beat of the blues. Having had sushi for lunch on Air Japan, we were all bored and still hungry. Especially Daddy. He did not eat any of the food, saving his palate politeness for times when he would not have paid hundreds of dollars for the privilege of eating raw fish. Out the window the ocean was covered with clouds that looked like Aunt Esther's white bedspread.

I reached for my new wallet, counting once again my new-found riches from going-away presents, and took out the pictures that Mr. Anderson had taken of the Cedar Avenue gang. I propped up the picture of Michelle on the little tray and scrunched down in my seat to look at her. She could iron, she could keep house, she loved the Lord. I would come back for her. My chest was heavy, like when Conrad sat on it and would not get up till I cried uncle.

Mother looked over at me, "What are *you* looking at?"

"Michelle."

"You are too young to be looking at her picture like that. It's not good. Why don't you read a book?"

"I don't feel like it," I said as the plane deepened into blue.

"You can't dwell on your feelings, Danny. You need to have a happy heart. Jesus will be with us, and you will make new friends in Vietnam."

Her disapproval was thick—no girlfriends and no homesickness allowed. We are happy about serving Jesus. I carefully put the picture back in my wallet (it was going to have to last a long time) and turned my head to the bedspread of clouds below.

On the trip over we were supposed to decide where I was to go to school. We visited Morrison Academy in Taiwan and Faith Academy in Manila, schools for missionary kids who were abandoned so that their parents could serve the Lord somewhere else. I strongly rejected the idea of being dropped off along the way. My decision came the first night in Manila when the adventure began to wear off and I started getting too homesick to ignore—my chest heaving the bed springs up and down in a loud squeak.

We arrived at the Christian and Missionary Alliance guest house at 327 Vo Tanh Street in Saigon after stopping in Japan, Taiwan, Hong Kong, the Philippines, Indonesia, and Singapore. We entered a large room with two beds, a dresser, a chair, a ceiling fan that wobbled slightly off center, and a bath shared with another missionary couple. Dumping the suitcases on the floor with travelers' relief, we plopped on the beds, finally here. Almost instantly I jumped up—too restless to be still. I walked to the yellow walls and opened the green slatted shutters. Traffic below on Vo Tanh Street darted back and forth. The breeze brought an incredible wash of sounds that I had heard in other cities on our way over, but these were now supposed to be *my* sounds. A smell was in the air that I had never smelled anywhere else—a strong smell of dead fish, but not of rot. The street lights were on, and there was an orange cast to the spots of light on the street complementing the yellow haze from the light bulb swinging in our room. The orange and yellow lights formed swaying shadows on the inside and the outside walls.

In the distance was another sound. I heard it at first as though it was underneath the sounds of bicycle bells and market bargaining. Then I heard it distinctly, a rumble, like high thunder over purple mountains' majesty. The strangeness of the room and the eerie tension of the approaching night felt like a tumor in my throat, growing slowly and choking the life out of me, cutting me off from oxygen breathed or water swallowed. This was too far to travel. My taffy-sweet life could not be stretched this far, and it broke into two pieces, each side dangling free from the other.

We arrived but had no plans. No place to live. Daddy did not know his job description. No salary. We were here by faith, blind faith, trusting that the churches who promised to send us money to support us actually would. Blessed are those who do not see and yet believe. Yet it was not only Jesus I could not see, it was tomorrow. It was a future. Life shrank small enough to be totally contained within those yellow missionary walls. Life ended right here. Tonight. I would just fade into the future and drift, because there was no destination, and even if there were, there was no map showing how to get there. The path was gone, the cycle of life, the things that made life orderly and allowed it to progress through time. Back to school, the World Series, the fall missions conference, Thanksgiving, Christmas, spring training, Easter, Memorial Day picnic, my birthday, and the Fourth of July. None of it was here. And there was nothing to replace it but the rising terror in my chest as I stared out the window.

Saigon

September 1967– February 1968

3
The Phoenix Study Group

Saigon, South Vietnam

It is morning and it is pretty early for my blood, about seven or so. I am sitting in the very back of an orange-and-white Volkswagen bus behind the last seat on the little shelf above the engine. It was the last seat available in the car pool. Everyone in the van knew everyone else, and all were in their regular seats in the passenger section. From my vantage point I had an immediate view out the back window. Keeping my head turned away from the kids in front of me, I watched the traffic envelop us. Smoking motorcycles revved their engines just inches away, blue-and-yellow taxis honked and swerved first to the right and then to the left, seeking any small advantage, and strange bicycle-looking things with little motors sitting on top of the front tire followed. The sky was blue-gray, and the engine beneath was vibrating up through my tail bone. I looked down at my clothes, suddenly aware of my shoes and notebooks and lunch. The day before we had made a trip to an outdoor market where we bought a translucent yellow plastic water container for me to tote to school. Everything here was plastic—from sandals to water bottles. I didn't know then how warm and foul the water would taste by lunch time.

I was picked up at the Christian and Missionary Alliance guest house at 327 Vo Tanh Street, where we were living while looking for a place of our own. Turning in and out of narrow streets, the bus stopped a few times after picking me up. At each stop Vietnamese maids would see off white children emerging from behind black iron gates set into high yellow walls. The walls had pieces of broken glass bottles cemented into the top, and these pieces protruded ragged-jagged. I don't remember anything about these kids except that they knew each other and they all knew their seats in the whiny bus. They were all talking about things that I didn't know about. Strange things. Suddenly I clearly saw a picture of Engvall Junior High School with the fog rolling over the top of the eucalyptus trees, and I was waiting in line talking to Todd. Here I knew what to talk about. Wait! It is no longer here, but there. Here is Saigon, and I do not know what to talk about.

The bus braked sharply and rolled me off balance. We had stopped in front of a narrow three-story building. The missionary mother/driver came around the back and unlocked the hatch while all the rest of the kids scrambled out the sliding side door and ran inside. I trailed her inside and was shown up three flights of tile stairs to a little room on the top floor. I found myself in the eighth grade at the Phoenix Study Group in Saigon.

Since I was starting school a little late, I got the last desk, one of two that constituted the front row. The room was minuscule compared to the ones back home designed for thirty or more kids. It was maybe ten by ten with two windows, a three-bladed ceiling fan, one old woman teacher and sixteen eyes behind me. Next to our room was another room, with the seventh grade in it. That room had a doorway that led out to a long balcony with wrought iron screening us in from floor to ceiling. The balcony looked over a busy four-lane street in Saigon, and we would spend recess all lined up looking down at the street, a few American kids held prisoner in Vietnam while the rest of Saigon slithered past on its motorbike way. The best recesses were when a military convoy of Americans would go by.

At the first sight of a jeep we all yelled really loud to see if we could get the attention of the GIs riding along on top of the tanks. Occasionally one would look up and see a sea of little American kids waving and calling and screaming at him. Then all the GIs would shout and whoop and holler and wave back.

Sometimes we would shout out the states we were from, "California!" "Missouri!" "Texas!" "New York!" and they would shout back "Georgia!" "Minnesota!" "Pennsylvania!" Then they would disappear behind one more concrete wall with miscellaneous broken coke bottles on top, and I would go back and sit in class, a little happier and a little more home-sick at the same time.

I sat next to the class genius. He was so smart that his parents had made arrangements with the teacher for him to have double homework every night. He kept a secret journal, and this gave him more social power here than any genius ever had at Engvall. He documented every fight, story, and event that happened in and around the eighth grade. There were secrets on those pages that kept the other kids, even those who would be most likely to trouble geniuses, at a respectful dis-tance. Besides the genius, there were the class criminal, the class clown, and, of course, the girls, whom, from the amount of make-up they wore, I immediately lumped together as unlikely candidates for suitable pastors' wives. In this small class of nine the social stakes were immediate and, once estab-lished, permanent. Having arrived late, I got dubbed the new kid and was relegated toward the bottom of the scale. This position was reinforced by other factors as well. Primarily, besides being more secular, they were all rich kids. Some even drove their own motorcycles to school and then would go downtown to mess around after school. Oil companies, engi-neering companies, and construction companies had sent their parents over, and they were making big bucks. My fam-ily, on the other hand, was there by faith. No set salary, just whatever people donated to the Pocket Testament League and requested be sent to our support. Along with our monthly check, PTL would send along a list of the donors' names and addresses so we could be properly thankful.

I immediately saw the need for a motorcycle, a red-and-cream Honda 50, to be exact. Daddy did not. The traffic alone was enough to make him rule out that possibility with the finality of God's eternal decrees. Of course, there were also all those rumors that "bad cowboys" rode up alongside Americans and cut their hands off to steal the watch. But I still asked whenever I thought I had caught him in a weakened mood. Daddy was never weak. A mixed blessing. Finally, after one too many conversations about it, exasperated, he made me a deal.

"Tell you what, Pal," he said, "If we ever get a thousand dollars support in one month you can get a Honda."

He might as well have said I could get one the next time we saw the Northern Lights in Saigon, because a thousand dollars was more than double our usual monthly income. Daddy almost choked when several churches sent us special one-time Christmas support gifts and our support for December just cracked the magic number. It was to no avail.

Without a motorcycle, of course, I could not do what the other kids did, which according to classroom tales and recorded in the genius's secret notebook, was go to each others' houses, steal drinks out of their mothers' liquor cabinets, and cause trouble for the Vietnamese, whom they universally detested. From the secret and official journal of all these proceedings the genius would sometimes relate to me some of the major crimes the kids had committed. This scared me as much as it intrigued me. Back home we built a few forts where we weren't supposed to, but we had never even broken a window in vandalism. These guys seemed to break and enter and steal things for the fun of it.

Our teacher was a retired American school teacher who was either looking for adventure or was out of her mind to be in this classroom. Her hair was short and silvery, and her rounded abdomen was the only part of her front that disturbed the line of her straight dresses. Her attempts at control were sometimes effective, and there would occasionally be enough quiet to diagram a sentence or follow a math problem. She mostly emphasized social studies, since we were right in the middle of one, and always had us read *Newsweek* magazine and then write about it every week.

Writing about an article in *Newsweek* was maddening—there were articles on every page. Living in Saigon was beginning to break up my nicely constructed suburban view of the world, and this assignment helped me along. Articles about Germany, Malaysia, or Egypt all seemed more real now. Just last year we had studied South America in seventh grade home room at Engvall, and I still remembered that Brazil speaks Portuguese and not Spanish. But the places didn't seem real no matter how many flags I colored, maps I numbered, or customs I raised my eyebrows at. Now all those places seemed real, the smells of Vietnam somehow awakening the rest of the world to me. It was America that seemed remote and vague. The memories of Pinecrest Drive and Cedar Avenue Baptist Church and Todd and Harley and Michelle seemed real but they now existed in another part of me that was becoming less real, dissolving in form, dimming in clarity. *Newsweek* articles about the States seemed to describe a semi-real place, just the way social studies used to. But now the rest of the world seemed real and the States resided over the horizon.

This place was right in my face, confronting me, challenging me, taunting me, demanding my attention and my energy. Home became real only at night when I lay in bed crying, breaking into little pieces, and wanting to see my brother Conrad so badly that I made a hundred oaths to God—oaths that if I could share a room with him again I would not hide his clothes, taunt his dates out of the window, or secretly daub on his Jade East cologne when he wasn't looking. God didn't seem interested in these oaths. He must have stayed in San

Bruno, because I never heard from him in Saigon. Daddy continued to hear regularly though, and that was enough to keep me trying those oaths in the helicoptered night.

I never made friends with any of these people at the Phoenix Study Group though the teacher went to the same church as we did in Saigon. The International Church was a generic evangelical church for all the missionary families who lived in Saigon. It had an assortment of chaplains, soldiers, and visitors each Sunday, but most of us were American missionaries with some Aussies and Brits thrown in. The teacher took me aside one day at school and told me that she did not believe what Daddy was teaching in Sunday school on powers of evil, like Satan and demons. Daddy thought she was a nice old lady but unwilling to accept clear biblical references to evil because she was afraid to. Her ignorance of how the world really worked was the topic of disdain and sarcastic humor among Mother, Daddy, and me. Poor old woman, she was as bad off as those liberal missionaries who could not figure out how those superstitions could remain so powerful in the light of such good education. Brother! They had no concept of the powers of darkness. How anyone could have trouble seeing the reality of evil in the midst of Saigon I'll never know.

Unlike my friends at Pinecrest, here my classmates and I never played together or even once saw each other outside of school. Unlike my friends at Cedar Avenue Baptist, there was never a baseball game to be played or a meeting to go to together. In San Bruno, life was pretty much a trinity of church, neighborhood, and school. Here that trinity broke into distinct and unrelated pieces. But the neighborhood was still the same in relation to church: they were the unsaved, and we were the saved.

4
Neighbors

Saigon, South Vietnam

Phu was fifteen. He was born somewhere in the middle of the Nguyen family with a pack of kids both above and below him. The oldest brother was studying aeronautical engineering in Germany, and his picture reclined on a little table in the dining room. He was coming home next year to be a fighter pilot in the Vietnamese Air Force. There was an older sister still at home who was studying French literature and upon whom I almost bestowed one of my famous crushes. I would have, but she didn't flirt with me as much as all the college-age girls at Cedar Avenue Baptist had when I was little, bringing me presents and having me sit on their laps at singspiration. I guess I was getting too old, and anyway, girls my own age were getting interesting lately. Especially Michelle Bonadelle, whose brown-eyed memory I carried with me, right under the New Testament in my shirt pocket. Phu had a brother just younger than I, Huong, and two more younger sisters who kept to the kitchen. Phu and Huong were my Vietnamese friends. I also had the Littleton kids—Stan, Pam, and Nora. Between the Littletons and the Nguyens I retained my balance of church kids and neighborhood kids. But it was Phu, Huong, and I who spent most afternoons prowling the riverbank, listening to the radio, and exploring each other's worlds.

Behind the Nguyen house there was a factory that converted Vespas to three wheeled taxis. Behind the factory was a branch of the Saigon river. At one time a road had been planned to go across a bridge to a little island in the fork of the river. The bridge had been built but not the road. That was good enough for us, though: it put us several hundred yards away from the house and gave us a space. Much like the eucalyptus trees in San Bruno, this round piece of ground with water flowing on all sides was a place that brought sense to my life. It was here we talked about religion and about victory in war and with a battery-operated phonograph listened and sang to the haunting tones of House of the Rising Sun. It was here I learned Vietnamese and here that I learned that as different as American and Vietnamese could be, our differences were bridged by friendship and dreams.

The first day we moved in, Phu gave me a tour of the grounds. We circled the factory, looking at the workbenches and stacks of crutches, and Phu warned me to stay away from the machinery in the back room. It was almost cool inside. The light filtered in through little holes in the wall and danced on particles of dust as they made their way to the sawdust floor. Rounding the back door, I almost stepped on an old man. He was hunched over in the shade, but his hands were working in a patch of sunlight. With a chisel in one hand and a very small hammer in the other, he was carving lattice-work details in a large screen. I looked for a moment before it took shape as a huge peacock. Feathers floated across bridges and streams, and flowers covered the ensembled screens for nearly twenty feet.

Phu said, "This is Tang; he is one of the finest wood carvers in all of Vietnam. He was very famous in Hanoi, and when we fled we brought him with us." I crouched down and Tang looked up at me with yellowed eyes, betel-juiced lips, and very few teeth. The wrinkles in his face were beyond belief. I had never seen a more wrinkled face in my whole life, and I had seen a lot of old people at funerals and nursing homes and prayer meetings. I kept looking at his wrinkles till he smiled and motioned to the screen and said, "Heh?"

"Very beautiful," I said, "very beautiful."

Phu translated. Tang nodded, and then, with the exchange done, he returned to his chipping, making the teak curl up in tiny controlled rills, leaving one more feather floating.

This was a good place to live, and we were lucky to have it. Getting it had been different from getting the Pinecrest house. There we had simply picked out a model, signed some stuff, and moved in. Getting things done over here was not so simple. When Daddy had been the pastor of a church in the States he could get done just about anything he wanted by the simple exertion of his will, even if that included helping church members see things the right way. Life in Saigon was a process of negotiations, a maze of relationships reflected through trick mirrors and cultural rules often buried in bureaucracy. In fact, things were not always what they seemed. The Phoenix Study Group was not a school; that would be illegal. It was just small groups of students with books explained by adults for a small monthly membership fee. The Crusader was owned by and registered to World Vision, even though it was paid for by donations to PTL and we had complete control of it. Jake Littleton was with the Christian and Missionary Alliance, but he was on loan to PTL, although with Daddy now here he mixed duties with the C&MA. Our translator, Trang, was on the team of Vietnamese pastors (we called them "nationals") whom PTL saw as central to their ministry even though Daddy was brought in as the regional director. Between the presence of national pastors in PTL, the hygiene relief packets from World Vision, and the long tradition of C&MA in Vietnam we gained access to many places where no one else could. It was in this mesh of obligations, loans, favors, and contracts that we heard about the possibility of an apartment.

World Vision had a contract with a family on the out-
skirts of Saigon in the district of Gia Dinh, which owned what
had formerly been a furniture factory. It now produced hundreds of crutches, canes, and wheelchairs for World Vision to
distribute in hospitals and military camps. The owner, Mr.
Nguyen, had a huge house next to the factory and wanted to
rent out part of the top floor. Not being part of a large company that provided housing, or even a mission board that
salaried its missionaries so they could afford small mansions,
we had to fend for ourselves. One day after school we drove
out to meet the Nguyens with our semi-official entourage of
Trang and Jake Littleton to underscore our respect and the
importance of the event. Besides, we needed interpreters.

This house was indeed a mansion. It was a two-story
white house with a red tile roof surrounded by verandahs and
nestled in a grove of coconut palms. To its side ran a long
metal building that was the crutch factory. The house sat well
back off the main road, its property running all the way back
to the Saigon River where, about two hundred yards upriver,
was the Bien Hoa bridge. The house seemed peaceful and
serene. At the top of the tile stairs sat a large room about fifteen by forty feet, with two little rooms on the end. One of
these was to be converted into a bathroom, if we would pay for
half the cost of its construction, and one was to be my bedroom. A door in the corner led to what would be my parents'
bedroom. At the other end of the room were paned doubled
doors that opened out onto a half-circle balcony overlooking
a grassy courtyard. This long room was the god-room, but if
we rented it, they would move the gods to the other side of the
house. The plan was finalized by agreeing to convert the
garage underneath into a kitchen.

Privacy was the big issue once we moved in. The kitchen
walls did not go all the way up to the ceiling and both the
Nguyens and the Peters could hear everything on either side
of the wall. The same was true upstairs. Mother and Daddy's

bedroom wall encased a large panel of window slats that opened onto a hallway in the Nguyens' side. Originally the slats had been installed to be dialed open to allow air to flow to the interior of the house. Now, although they remained closed, they kept out no sound. We were actually living in the Nguyens' house. The smell of nuc mum and incense drifted in and out, as did the tides of conversation and chatter in Vietnamese. We, of course, remained as quiet as possible.

Sometimes I would spend an evening on the Vietnamese side of the slatted wall watching *Combat* reruns on their TV. We would sit in straight-backed hand-carved wooden chairs all lined up in a row—Phu, Huong, Mr. Nguyen, and I—our faces flickering in green. Phu knew more about American TV than I did, and this always made me feel funny because I felt a sense of ownership over the programs. These were my programs from my country. But Phu knew more about the shows and plots and characters than I did.

"Do you remember the one where Savage was wounded and hid in the barn?" he asked hopefully.

I answered in a flattened but superior tone, "No."

San Bruno

Our next-door neighbors at 2130 Pinecrest Drive were the Hampshires. Dougie Hampshire had something we only occasionally had—a TV—and I would often watch it at his house, especially cartoons in the afternoon, since I had to be home by the time the evening shows came on. Once I thought I had finally worked out a deal with my parents to spend Thursdays with a friend from church watching TV.

"Do they just watch the *family* shows?" Mother asked.

"Yes, Mrs. Walden said they *only* watch the *family* shows," I said, lightly salting the word *family* with moral emphasis.

Mother relented, and I was ready to watch my favorite, *My Three Sons*, now on a weekly basis. The whole plan fell through when I discovered that the Walden's definition of family shows was limited to nature and travel programs and the news. Ugh, I hated *Wild Kingdom* and that white-haired guy's fake adventures. I was going to have to be satisfied with cartoons at the Hampshires.

It was at the Hampshires, watching cartoons, that I learned the difference between our house and other houses. Dougie and I were sprawled on the new rug, which was so big it almost went to the corners of the room, when his brother, the neighborhood hood, Harold, came in. They were just about as far apart in age as Conrad and I were, though they were both a little younger. Harold's face was red and he started screaming at Dougie.

"What did you do with my notebook?" he yelled.

Before Dougie could whine, Harold leaped over the back of the couch and headed for us. Dougie, having experienced these attacks before, spun around and ran out of the room, with Harold breathing down his neck, screaming, "Where is it, you little pus mouth rat? Where is it?"

Fortunately for Dougie, the dining room, kitchen, and living room were in an open U shape, and one could run around and around forever. It was impossible for Harold to trap him, especially given his bulk and Dougie's quickness. Around and around they ran, never stopping screaming and finally bringing Mrs. Hampshire out from the back of the house. Just the sight of his mother enraged Harold out of his already crazed head. On his last run through the kitchen he stopped suddenly. Dougie stopped in the living room, and I saw absolute hate for Harold in his eyes.

With a primal scream, Harold flung himself around the corner toward Dougie with a big butcher knife in his hands. I froze. Dougie did not. Mrs. Hampshire let out a hysterical yell and joined the race, all three chasing each other around. Mrs. Hampshire chased Harold chasing Dougie around and around.

Mrs. Hampshire yelled, "Harold, you put down that knife this instant, do you hear me?"

Harold yelled, "I'm gonna kill 'im!"

Dougie yelled, "You can't catch me!"

Mrs. Hampshire yelled, "Wait till your father gets home. I will have him whip you with the strap."

Harold yelled, "Shut up!"

By this time I had given up on Rocky and Bullwinkle and was standing up in a corner of the living room, eyeing the front door. I couldn't get past the fray, and I knew to stay out of Harold's way on any day and especially today. Finally the three squared off at three of the four corners of the pink Formica kitchen table and stared at each other, all screaming together. "I gotta go," I said and darted out the front door, tore down the front steps two at a time, and ran home.

Breathlessly bursting through the front door, I entered a totally different world. Momoo was at the stove stewing tomatoes and listening to KEAR, the Christian radio station. George Beverly Shea was singing at a Billy Graham crusade the soft notes of "The Ninety and Nine." I sank into the rocking chair and caught my breath. We were different from them. This was our house. That was who they were, and that was their house. Our house had no chaos. Daddy's presence brought it a sense of well-ordered peace.

Daddy was the head of 2130 Pinecrest Drive. There was no doubt about it, but he was never too autocratic. There was always a softness in his eyes when he looked at me and a tenderness of heart that drew me to sit on his lap and walk holding his hand until I was too old. Either there was little rebellion in the house because there was little discipline, or there was little discipline in the house because there was little rebellion. While his authority was never in doubt, in many ways he and Mother were quite a team and that kept things together.

Mother would say, "I'll have to talk to Daddy about it," and Daddy would say, "I'll have to talk to Mother about it." They were such a team that it was impossible to play one against the other. I learned this once on vacation when, having been turned down by Daddy, I asked Mother if I could buy a souvenir six-shooter. This appeared to be working just fine until we got to the car and I pulled that deadly gun out of the bag.

"Where'd you get that gun, Pal?" Daddy suddenly asked.

I was dead; I'd shot myself. Good thing I was a Christian already. "Mother said I could have it," I tentatively bargained.

He put his hand across the back of the front seat and twisted around to face me directly.

"Pal, if either of us says no to something, you cannot ask the other one for it. Is that clear?"

The tone of his voice clarified any doubts I might have at one time in my life been susceptible to, and I mumbled something in shamed response.

"All right, let's hit the road," he said. He turned out of the store's parking lot onto a two-lane road and began singing, the crisis taken care of and disappearing behind us now.

After a whipping like that, I just stared at the gun. I did not want it anymore. I dropped it on the floor and lay down on the seat. I propped my feet up on the door handle and looked out the back window at the tree tops blurring by.

If you could not play them against each other, it was not surprising, for the most amazing thing was that they never fought. I never in all my years heard an angry word between them. Anger was not allowed in the first place, it being the enemy of sweetness and kindness, which was how we were supposed to feel on the inside and act on the outside. Like Jesus, they saved anger only for outrages at unrighteousness. Mother and Daddy took great pride in having never fought, and Daddy had counseled many people, telling them that the answer was very simple.

"A marriage that is 50–50 will fail," he counseled. "That is the problem with marriages today, they are based on 50–50 commitment. Instead of it adding up to 100 percent, what you really get is two half-committed people in a half-baked marriage, and it will fail every time." "No," Daddy would repeat, "the right way to have a marriage is 100–100. Each person must give 100 percent to the other person 100 percent of the time."

Mother and Daddy played the 100–100 rule perfectly, I guess, because they never fought. They did disagree once, though, and it ended up causing me a lot of grief.

"It is impossible, here on God's fallen earth, for a man and a woman to live together for a lifetime and not fight. And I mean fight!" Evangelist Feldman hollered. "Amen?" he asked.

Reverend Dale Feldman was an old friend of Daddy's from Moody Bible Institute days and was that fall's evangelist. He was more conservative than we were and had very strict ideas about family behavior. Daddy had not heard him preach for many years and did not know that his new style was to yell for an hour every night on how bad it was for engaged couples to kiss and that brothers should never wear T-shirts around the house in front of their sisters. On the third unfortunate night of this five-day revival he had preached enthusiastically and at length about marriage and kept repeating one point over and over again.

The church, familiar with the sweetness of Mother and Daddy's marriage, remained quiet at the repeated requests for an Amened response. This seemed to agitate the evangelist all the more, and he intensified his claims and argued and sweated through Genesis, Proverbs, and the apostle Paul. By the time he finished he must have thought this church had gone liberal, for there was not much agreement. Daddy closed with a quick hymn at the altar call (which brought nobody down the aisle) and a perfunctory prayer.

Daddy and I were driving Reverend Feldman back to his hotel down on El Camino when, in an unusual move, Daddy cleared his throat and confronted his ol' but mistaken buddy on the necessity of fighting marriages. It was after three blocks of sweaty silence that Daddy began.

"Dale," Daddy started, "you are flat wrong on this thing. There is, first, no biblical evidence for it. Second, it flies in the face of reason. What is to keep a man and a woman from a life-time of love? Third, I know better (this is where Daddy had the strained evangelist nailed) because Rube and I have never ever, not once in twenty-three years, fought one time. Not once! We have never even raised our voices at each other. If each partner is giving 100 percent, it won't happen."

"John," the evangelist responded, "are you telling me that you have never . . ."

Before he could finish his sentence a memory flooded over me, and, always allowed to enter adult conversations, I interrupted to tell the story.

"Daddy, you and Mother did have a fight once. Remember when you were lost in San Francisco and you wanted to go left and Mother wanted to go right? It was right by that rail-road crossing where Mr. Bask has his print shop."

"Pal, that was not an argument. We were just discussing it together."

"No, Daddy, I remember." Then I imitated Mother's voice saying, "'Johnny, we have already been that way. It is down here on the right where we double back.' Don't you remember, Daddy?"

"Pal," Daddy remonstrated in an embarrassed way, "Mother and I have never fought."

At this I became insistent about the truth, repeating the details until Daddy finally told me to just be quiet, finishing with "That's enough."

Evangelist Dale sat with a smirk on his face as Daddy got out of the car to buy four dozen mixed donuts for tomorrow morning's dawn prayer meeting. After we dropped the evan-gelist off at the motel, we drove home in thick silence. Daddy was upset at the discussion with Dale. His moment of proof was destroyed by my memory, and there was nothing he could do about it. One of us appeared to be lying. The tension in the car poked me in the lungs as I stifled a cry. Before Daddy had the car fully parked in front of the house, I ran inside and climbed up into my top bunk. I was lying there in the dark crying when I heard him come in with a long sigh. He stood next to my bunk and laid his head down next to mine. He smelled like the pulpit and there was stale coffee on his breath.

"I'm sorry, Daddy; I thought it was a fight and I thought I should tell the truth."

"Ahh, Pal, it doesn't matter what ol' Dale thinks anyway. If you think that discussion was the sole example of Mother and me fighting, then it's okay with me, because that wasn't any fight. You have never heard people get angry with each other and talk mean to each other. You don't even know what that is like, Pal."

"It wasn't a fight?"

"No," Daddy laughed. "It was a disagreement, though; but we were not angry or anything."

"I'm sorry, Daddy."

"It was just a misunderstanding. I love you, Pal," he said as he hugged me to him. "Why don't you pull those clothes off and get ready for bed? We've got to be at church at 5:30. You want to come with me?"

"If I can get up," I sniffed. "I always try but I can't get up."

"That's all right. You need your sleep anyway. Night, Pal."

After everybody had gone to bed, I heard the low drone of Daddy's voice coming through the wall. Mother and Daddy were talking about the event. I slithered out of bed and stooped in the back of the closet, my ear to the wall to see if I could hear something. I couldn't. I had never heard any actual words with the closet method, just the up and down of tired tides from the day's last words.

It was several months later that I got one of my few actual spankings, and through that experience I learned more about fighting and nonfighting families. We knew that the Hampshires needed the Lord. You could tell from the scream-ing, swearing, spitting, and screwdriver throwing. We were having a revival at church and, off and on, we could get Dougie or Harold to come. This Wednesday night Harold had come and apparently even listened. He seemed to be in a reflective mood as we rode in the back seat, dropping neigh-borhood kids off on the way home. After the last kid was dropped off, Harold and I shared the back seat while Mother drove alone in the front. I was feeling close to Harold that night. He seemed sad, and I was not afraid of him.

"Harold," I said, "you know your dad drinks and smokes. Don't you wish he was a Christian and didn't do those things?"

"I like my dad," he said.

"Yeah, but don't you wish he was like Daddy?"

"That's enough, Danny," Mother warned. But for some reason I was on a mission here to help Harold see the truth. His dad was bad, whereas mine was good. It was simple and pure and nurtured my insistence.

Undaunted by Mother's caution, though perhaps driving this witnessing thing down a wrong street, I accelerated, "But Harold, you know your dad drinks *beer!* Ugh, that stinks! Daddy would never drink beer; he's a Christian."

Harold growled back now, "My dad is just fine the way he is."

"Harold, he can't be fine," I retorted, sure of my moral ground. "Wouldn't you just rather have my dad than your dad?"

Mother almost snapped at me. "Danny!"

I was finally finding my point, this was not about his dad being a Christian; Daddy was just simply better than his dad. This was my version of my dad can beat up your dad—with a fundamentalist twist: my dad is more righteous than your dad!

We pulled up in front of the house, and Harold sprang from his back seat prison of accusations and lumped home. Self-confident at the truth of all I had said but somehow tight inside, I followed Mother in. I was in the kitchen rummaging through the icebox when I heard Daddy call.

"Pal, will you come in here, please?"

I walked in and found the living room filled with an air of trouble, and it was about to settle on me.

"What did you say to Harold in the car, Pal?"

My skin clammed up all over, and I suddenly remembered Mother's warnings to stop talking. "I dunno."

"Did you say his dad drank beer and wasn't a Christian and that didn't he think he would rather have me for a dad?"

"Yeah. But it's true and ... "

"Pal, you can never attack people that way and you can never disobey your Mother. Do you understand?"

"Yeah, but ... "

"I am going to have to spank you. Come here."

Daddy put me over his knee and spanked me. I cried instantly even though he had never spanked me hard or for long. After a few swats I got up and went to my room, leaving a wet spot the size of a quarter on his blue suit. I cried in my pillow and waited for him to come in and talk to me. The next day he went over and apologized to Mr. Hampshire for my bad attitude. I apologized to Harold, but he never came back to church.

Saigon

It was when Mr. Nguyen got drunk one night that I lay in bed and listened to him scream at his family and remembered the Hampshires. There was no way out here, no home to run to, just this room in the middle of other rooms where our family could not be separate from theirs. Something smashed on the other side of the wall and crashed, breaking on the floor. One of the girls screamed in response, and somebody else began sobbing. Footsteps pounded down the stairs and fear seeped through the slats. Daddy just lay there too. There was nothing either of us could do but listen and shake with the house itself.

The next morning Daddy told me to tell Phu to tell his father that if it ever happened again we would move out immediately. Hearing that news, Mr. Nguyen paid us a visit that afternoon. He knocked quietly at the door, and Daddy, seeing him through the window, went to open the door himself.

"I am sorry," Mr. Nguyen said.

"Mr. Nguyen," replied Daddy, "you realize that we cannot tolerate that behavior. I will not allow my family to be subject to that."

"Yes, yes, I am very sorry." Then pointing to his head he said, "It gets bad here. Very bad here."

"No," Daddy said, gently tapping Mr. Nguyen on the middle of his chest, "The problem is not in your head, it is here, in your heart. There will never be peace in your head until there is peace in your heart, which only God can give."

"I am sorry," Mr. Nguyen said quietly.

"Never again," said Daddy.

5
Naked Ladies

Saigon

The eighth grade at the Phoenix Study Group was different in many ways from Engvall Junior High in San Bruno, California. One of the more important differences was the lanky girl with the straight brown hair, who not only could draw pictures of naked ladies but actually did draw pictures of naked ladies on the chalkboard when the teacher was out of the room. This emerging artist would draw long swoopy lines that, with the final sweep of chalk, magically emerged as legs, hips, and torso of a reclining nude. I tried not to look shocked. Actually, I tried to just not look. I managed the first better than the second. That was because I had, of course, seen pictures of naked ladies before—once.

San Bruno

As usual, it was a breezy wet day in San Bruno, the edge of a gray fog bank breaking off into high chunks and sailing over the heads of the neighborhood gang. We were coming back from playing baseball at the top of the hill, baseball bats slung over our shoulders, old gloves on our hands. Walking right down the middle of the street, we were feeling the power that all great athletes feel, so we did not notice at first, our vision still cluttered with line drives and road-skinned baseballs, but then, we did notice. The street, each little rock dipped in black and damp from fog, was littered with dozens of pictures of naked ladies. Somebody, probably Harold the neighborhood hood, had thrown a deck of cards out of a passing car's window. I had heard at school that you could buy these in Chinatown along with other illegal goods, particularly firecrackers and switchblades. This was one of those packs of cards that had red and black shapes on one side and on the flip side a picture of a lady—a naked lady—sitting on an orange or green pillow. Both sides interested me.

It was a "well-known fact" that when a gambler got saved, a Las Vegas real-thing gambler, the first thing he would do, not the second thing he would do, was to throw away his pack of cards because they were anti-Christ. Do not confuse this with the Antichrist in the Great Tribulation. That is sort of the Devil himself. All playing cards were just the Devil's way of mocking Christ. It was another "well-known fact" that the Joker was Christ and that each card symbolized a hidden anti-Christ meaning. To play cards was to mock the Savior and laugh at him foolishly, just like the demons in hell—even though they believe and tremble. So, it was pretty interesting to see those black and red shapes.

But then there was the other side—the naked-lady side. This seemed to confirm the rumor that these cards could be bought in Chinatown, because all the naked ladies had straight black hair, yellow skin, and big brown nipples. Exotic naked Asian ladies on the Devil's cards right down the middle of Pinecrest Drive.

Todd, Gary, Don, Rod, and Jack, and I ran zigzag from card to card picking them up like they were dollar bills. Then the dilemma set in. What should we do with them? Between the two sons of the Greek Orthodox priest, me the preacher's kid, and one of the others being the son of my Sunday school teacher, this was a major dilemma, because we prided ourselves on being good kids. Besides that, there was an ongoing competition over which religion was the best. Obviously, none of us could want to keep the immoral cards without sacrificing hard-won standing regarding the merits of being Baptist or Greek Orthodox or Catholic. After some confusion, we decided to take them to Rod's mom (the wife of my Sunday school teacher), since she was the only parent in the whole neighborhood at home. We traded the cards for a pat on the head, effusive praise for being good boys, and an apple. We were experienced in such trades due to our extensive background in baseball cards, although in this instance there was really no bargaining over the old card before it was traded away for something like a new Jim Ray Hart. I felt pretty good about it, though I would have felt better about getting chocolate and I was not quite finished looking at either side of the card.

Heading back outside, we were now consumed with something almost as interesting—the mystery. Throwing our bats and gloves on the grass, we avoided sitting down on the wet lawn, but instead hung out in various positions on the driveway throwing questions and theories at each other. How did they get in the street? Who did it? Why? This was a mystery worthy of us as we unnoticeably evolved from baseball players into private detectives. Sitting on the ledge separating the driveway and the lawn, we ate our apples deliberately, carefully considering the skin and the core as we put our heads to the task at hand. The mystery remained unsolved, but at least Harold the neighborhood hood was firmly at the top of our suspect list by the time we all had to go home.

Later that night, as I lay in the top bunk, I considered calling my brother Conrad on the bed phone. Our bed phone was an old vacuum cleaner hose, the kind with woven fabric stretched between two aluminum tubes, one of which attached to the head and the other to the skinny canister. Conrad had tied it to the bunk bed posts, and we could lie and talk very quietly to each other through the tube long after we were supposed to be asleep. It smelled of dust and old rugs, and it left a taste in your mouth of some of the things that had lost their life to its suction. Having a brother seven years older was a real pain, especially for him. But he was good to pose certain questions to that I did not particularly want to ask Mother. I knew this because I had asked him what the Beatles' "hard day's night" meant—especially when on the school yard I had heard the added words, "under the covers." Looking almost alarmed, he said in a very serious tone, "Never, never say that again, Danny." But he did not scold me or pursue who said what to whom when and in what hallway, so I felt safe in exploring other dangerous places in the world with him. I lay in bed contemplating whether to tell him about the naked ladies. He might hear about it anyway and then ask me about it, and I would have to deny any knowledge of it. I felt strange all over. My brain raced with the Conrad question, my vision filled with naked ladies looking right back at me with those large eyes and rounded shoulders and delicate breasts. Before I could decide whether or not to talk to Conrad, I heard his regular breathing, so I just lay there with pictures of sugar plums dancing in my head, feeling the sheets stretched tightly over my skin.

The real picture of a real woman's real breast greatly increased my awareness and curiosity about the whole topic in general. The pictures seemed to fast-forward my consciousness about women. I always had girlfriends, between church, school, and neighborhood; they were omnipresent. If hating girls was in a particularly high tide on Pinecrest Drive, I usually had a girlfriend at church or vice versa. But seeing these cards heightened my general awareness of women, even at church. It is ironic, that it was at that citadel of morality, at church, that the possibility of seeing a real live breast first arose.

Mitch Gooden and Dutch Fines came flying around the corner in the basement hallway of the church and skidded to a halt in front me and the rest of the assembled boys from our Sunday school class. Panting and wild-eyed, Mitch told us that

Mrs. Miller was breast-feeding her new baby in the nursery and they had both seen her through the window. This was incredible. We all knew that the Millers were a little off, they wore rumpled clothes and went gold mining in the motherlode on some weekends and even missed church. But none of us had ever heard of anybody breast-feeding before. Having been nurtured on the much improved sterilized formula of the 1950s modern mother, our technologically advantaged minds could not possibly imagine that somebody would do it at church.

"No way, Mitch!" I said, "I don't believe you." That began an exchange of "Is tos" and "Is nots." After all, this was my father's church, and I knew he would not allow breast-feeding on the premises, or probably anywhere else for that matter. Before I could resort to the ultimate challenge of "Prove it!" Mitch beat me to it, calmly stating with a settled air that unsettled me, "If you don't believe me, all you gotta do is go around and look in the parking lot window."

This, of course, immediately challenged the limits of our strategic capabilities as a group of boy adventurers in an adult world, and certainly now, in a very real and dangerous situation.

"Listen," James whispered, "if we all go look at once, she will know what is going on and will cover up and we won't be able to see."

None of us said anything about what would be covered up and what we wouldn't be able to see but we were in silent agreement that we did not want that to happen. The gravity of the situation shifted the weight of the conversation away from whether or not it was really happening to how we were going to see it happening. This was too big an opportunity to miss. Who knows, maybe this was the only chance any of us would ever have to see a real woman's real breast.

Mitch suggested, "Just do what I did, stroll by sorta like you are looking for rocks in the flower bed, and then just look in."

More plans were discussed and rejected until Mitch got too impatient, "You idiots! At this rate she is going to be done before we look." It had not occurred to any of us that there was a time limit to this sort of thing, but he might be right. The looking-for-rocks-in-the-flower-bed approach was adopted. We would do it two at a time, in three shifts.

I was in the second group, Mitch and Dutch had a claim to be first since they had discovered the treasure. Fortunately, most of the adults were on the other side of the building, and we were safe for a few minutes. Who knew when a parent or a girl might show up? Mitch and Dutch walked so casually up to the window and looked in that I couldn't believe it. They moved past and then turned to us and nodded with deliberate and sober meaning. Bobby King and I were next. It was time. We walked forward, looking down at the red-turned-gray bark dust with its bits of black plastic curling up toward the hedge running along under the window. We did not get as close as Mitch and Dutch did, but close enough. The nursery was in a daylight basement so we could look down at an angle and see Mrs. Miller sitting behind the nursery split-door talking to Barbara, who was on nursery duty that day. It was true, Mrs. Miller was holding the baby to her chest. Unfortunately, she was covered from shoulder to waist by a white baby blanket with little pink flowers and a yellow border. We had come very close, but the actual discovery of this new world was not of much value. We reassembled at the far corner of the building, and the debate turned to whether or not she should be doing that in church. The consensus was definitely negative.

Saigon

So, you can see that when the lanky girl with the straight brown hair drew naked ladies on the board in the eighth grade class at the Phoenix Study Group I had quite a bit of experience in the whole field. That is to say I was experienced at pictures of breasts. I had still never seen a real one. In Saigon, this was soon to change.

As usual Daddy picked me up after school in The Crusader, and we went to do some errands. We had to go downtown and check our mail at JUSPOA to see if we had heard from the kids. Then it was time to get some more aluminum chloride for mother. She could not find any Ban roll-on deodorant, so she just smeared the chemicals straight on under her arms. We bought this stuff from a certain apothecary downtown, and that is where we were now headed. Finding a parking place for a two-ton Chevy panel truck in Cho Lon was never easy. Not driving a military truck, we could not just stop anywhere we pleased for hours on end, and not driving a moped, we could not just lean it up against a wall. Finally finding a parking place a few blocks away, we walked together back toward the store. It was on the far side of a small roundabout, and Daddy decided to circle it on the sidewalks rather than risk our lives by cutting straight across into the moving wall of bicycles and taxis in the street. Passing open storefronts filled with gutted ducks hanging still and Sony radios playing Chinese opera, we walked carefully through children squatting and dogs panting. The sidewalk circled the roundabout about two feet up off the street. Every time we came to a street or alley, we descended three steps, crossed, and then stepped back up to continue around the circle. It was while we were descending the steps to cross the widest street that I looked across the traffic and saw a lady sitting on the far sidewalk leaning against the front wall of a shop.

Her blouse was completely drooped around her waist, and she was holding a small baby. Then I knew. This was the day, here in the dieseled air of downtown Saigon, that I would see my first breast. Fearing that Daddy would change course or steer me away from the sight of her, I hung back half a step. As I crossed the street, preparing to get a good look, I knew that I should not look. I knew that I should straighten my shoulders and look straight ahead as would Daddy. But, unlike Daddy, I was usually round shouldered in situations like this.

Getting closer with each step, I felt excitement rise and my heart began pumping a little harder. I, Danny Peters, was about to look upon a real woman's real breast—that object of mystery, that sacred secret of the girls, the wonder of the universe, the highest of God's creation. After quick-stepping across the street between signals, we were mounting the stairs on the far side when suddenly Daddy stiffened in embarrassment, squared his shoulders, and looked straight ahead. At over six feet he could avoid this scene. At five feet there was no way I could, I was too close to the squatting woman.

With timing more precise than swinging at a baseball, I looked down and saw the face of a naked Vietnamese baby pointing up at me full in my own face. It was asleep, its head tilted backward over the crook in the woman's arm. The baby's eyes were closed, and a fly was feeding at the tear seeping from the left eyelid. It must have cried itself to sleep, for the breast was dry. The beggar woman's eyes searched my face while she held her hand out to me but I looked past it to see her breast. It lay like a piece of thin leather flat against her chest, its only form the outline of each jutted rib beneath. No more than an elongated flap of skin, it ended in a nipple cracked and dry and rimmed with dark lines. There was no fullness, no firmness, no flesh. No exotic naked Asian lady sitting on a green pillow with small shoulders and delicate breasts. My final reward in the search for the discovery of this new world, this ancient treasure found, this moment of secret joy that was to be mine at the moment when I was ready at the invitation of the universe to see the mysteries of life, flooded me with the presence of disease and death. I looked up and focused on the pinpoints of perspiration dotting the back of Daddy's white shirt and understood that he knew that I had looked and had seen. We handled it in the usual way we handled awkward situations. We walked away in embarrassed silence.

6
Snipers

Saigon

I don't remember how long we had been in Vietnam when Daddy turned The Crusader from a pot-holed street of dogs and dust into a driveway that led through an iron gate shouldered by two square concrete pillars. They were the color of all the square pillars in Vietnam, a yellow-almost-beige from years of fading in the Mekong sun. I do remember that it was a Sunday afternoon and we were coming from Tan Son Nhut Air Force Base, where we had eaten Sunday dinner at a big cafeteria. As an occasional correspondent for a missions magazine, he had been given press credentials and assigned the rank of major so he could fly on military planes and buy stuff on military bases—like real American food.

We didn't cook much at the apartment in Gia Dinh because we had a 2.5-cubic-foot refrigerator (just big enough for eleven cans of soda) and a two-burner hot plate. A water filter and a small table and chairs completed the kitchen. The kitchen was in a former garage. It had an oil-stained cement block floor and double garage doors, which we would leave wide open to look out onto the driveway as we ate. The negotiations for the apartment included the need for a kitchen and a bathroom. The kitchen was connected to the ex-god-room upstairs by cutting a hole in its floor and adding a set of wooden stairs, so narrow and so steep that they were really more like a ladder. Mother had to go carefully up and down to and from the kitchen, making sure her shoes and skirt did not get caught on the steps.

The Pinecrest kitchen had been nothing like this. Speckled Formica countertops enclosed a dual sink, where I filled water balloons in the summer, and a brown range top, where I made fried-egg sandwiches with ketchup and yolks that ran down my arms. Out of that kitchen's oven often came my favorite dish—a rectangular casserole of chicken, rice, peas, and cheese. The Pinecrest kitchen also had the official clock on the oven. At nine o'clock, by that clock, I had to go to bed. But the kitchen was different here. As a result of this Saigon kitchen arrangement, combined with the unavailability of normal food, or even a maid such as the other missionary families had for cooking the abnormal food, we ate a lot of canned food from the PX and a ton of stale Pop Tarts. I do not know why there were several thousand boxes of old Pop Tarts made available for relief distribution and for relief workers, but every day after school I crammed the dry paste into my mouth and washed it down with a soda. So, it is understandable that on certain choice Sundays we looked forward to some middle-class equilibrium at the cafeteria at Tan Son Nhut Air Force Base.

On those elect Sundays the long line of army green guys included a broad-shouldered, white-haired preacher in a gray suit, a small round woman in a print dress, and an awkward thirteen-year-old. Sliding our trays along those stainless steel tubes and being asked if we preferred fried chicken or roast beef had a marvelous effect on my search for a familiar sense of life. The cafeteria was clean and shiny and recognizable, all the way from the music in the background to the color of the servers' eyes. It was not as good as baking cookies in the Pinecrest kitchen, but somehow it worked almost as well. Even better, after slices of roast, piles of mashed potatoes, ladles of gravy, a slice of pumpkin pie, and cold, cold milk, we would sometimes go across the base to a showroom of all-American delights.

This showroom was sort of a hanger-turned-shopping-mall. Enterprising merchants displayed cameras and tele-scopes, suitcases and diamond rings, shoes and vacation plans. Best of all, there was a brand new 1968, white, four-door Chevy Biscayne. A real Chevy right here in Vietnam. GIs could sign up to buy one and have it waiting for them when they got home. I used to stand behind the green velour ropes, my hands in my pockets, and just look at it. The light bulbs overhead reflected in strangely elongated shapes on its bumpers and windows. The fenders curved in perfection, the taillights pure red. It was such a right-angled contrast to the funny blue and yellow kiddie cars that honked and hunkered everywhere else in Saigon. Here before me in a huge air-con-ditioned warehouse was a real car.

San Bruno

In San Bruno there had been many neighborhood debates over the merits of the cars owned by each family on the block. We had a 1960 two-door Le Sabre with a Wildcat engine and a Volkswagen. The Volkswagen counted for noth-ing in spite of Daddy's bemused protests at my disgust of it—"Pal, it's got four on the floor, bucket seats, an air-cooled engine, and a fast back!" All I could do was bury my head under the couch pillows and moan. The Buick was better, my only shot at neighborhood auto respectability. It had a pretty good ranking until we got it painted. Some time after we bought it, well used (as befitted Daddy's occupation), we had it painted at a discount place down on El Camino. This was in preparation for our big trip to see the relatives in St. Louis and to go on deputation to raise money for our support on the mission field. Mother had picked out a nice color called "Buick White," which she thought would go well with the grass green interior.

Unfortunately, the paint guys made a mistake, which was immediately obvious when we went to pick it up. With a seething but controlled presence, Daddy looked them straight in the eye. "We both know, sir, that *that* is not Buick White," he said pointing to a very long tail-finned and now turquoise Buick. The manager whined (a big mistake when talking to Daddy, I knew from experience). "That *is* Buick White . . . it just looks different when it's on the car." Proudly, I turned out to be the key player in this stand-off. I spied the disputed color sample lying on the manager's desk and picked it up. The freshly applied coat of turquoise came off on my fingers revealing creamy Buick White beneath. I elbowed Daddy and whispered, "Look at this." Danny Orlis himself, Christian boy detective, could not have done better. They were sunk and agreed to repaint the car the next week. Unfortunately we were leaving the very next day. Missionaries are not supposed to have good taste, but Daddy was horrified.

The trip and the parental mortification were not my biggest problems, however. A turquoise car with grass green interior left me pretty much out of contention for having the best car on the block, though I thought it was still better than the Todd's Plymouth station wagon, hemi or not.

Saigon

In Saigon, cars were completely different. I did not pay attention to all the nuances, though, since our car was now a forest green two-ton Chevy panel truck with "The Crusader" of Philadelphia College of the Bible stenciled on the door and "Tin Lanh" painted two feet high on the side. But when we would take an afternoon off and go to the shopping warehouse and see that Chevy, I remembered what a real car was.

This Sunday, having just come fresh from Sunday dinner and the Chevy showroom, I was feeling rather stuck in The Crusader as we headed over to visit GIs at a hospital on the other side of Saigon. It was into the hospital grounds that we turned through those faded yellow gates. An MP waved us past a little guard shack, and we followed the straight and narrow driveway to the end, where we parked in front of some rather forgettable one-story buildings. The grounds had a little grass here and a little dirt there, a limp flag, and a couple of guys in wheelchairs sitting off to one side under an aluminum awning. I first noticed the silence when getting out of the truck. As I slammed the door I heard the creak of the hinge and the rattle of the window play against a backdrop of no other noise. My Sunday shoes crunched loudly through small Army gravel as we walked toward a flight of three gray steps.

Once inside, we visited at the bedside of several soldiers, lying in bandages, subdued, quiet. I hung back at the foot of the bed, uneasy and squeamish at the sights and the smells and that still loud silence. There was no laughing, no banging or clanging, just the silence of the wounded afternoon. Most of the time I stayed outside, my parents never demanding me to perform and, in this case, allowing me some distance from them on this island of American safety.

I walked through the steam of Saigon that was drifting through the verandahs and looked away from the faces of the GIs, focusing instead on the chipped paint flaking off the multi-layered banisters. There was too much heaviness in their presence and too much hope in their eyes when they saw an American kid walk down the hall. Was I the mirage of their baby brother? What was I doing there? Would I talk to them just a little? My body was walking forward but I had spun a mental U-turn and descended a flight of internal stairs to a fort within, where I could spend time alone and keep my distance.

It was near the end of the afternoon, just as we were getting ready to leave, that a wounded soldier began a halting conversation with Daddy. He had a boyish face and light skin and looked too young to be here. Maybe he was nineteen. The whole top of his head was circled in bandages swooping down over his left eye and ear. He managed to tell us that the side of his head had been creased by a sniper's bullet as he patrolled up the Mekong River. It was obviously affecting his emotions, memories, motions, and words. Reaching into his pocket and fumbling out a worn blue aeroform, the wounded soldier's words stumbled out, "I got a letter from my wife and she is leaving me for somebody back home."

Daddy talked with him and shared the gospel with him, saying pastorally, "There is no peace on earth; there never will be, because human hearts are separated from God by sin. Only one Person can ever understand your grief. In Jesus Christ alone there is forgiveness and peace."

The wounded soldier said, "I got a letter from my wife and she is leaving me for somebody back home."

Daddy talked some more and then asked if he could pray.

The wounded soldier said, "I got a letter from my wife and she is leaving me for somebody back home."

Daddy prayed, "Heavenly Father, the ways of this world are beyond us. We do not understand the pain and the suffering in this young fella's life. We ask thee, O Father, that thou wouldst make yourself real to my new friend here and that he may find the reconciliation and the forgiveness and the peace brought through the cross of Christ. Turn our hearts toward you, Father, that we might trust you in the darkest hour and the blackest night. Father, we pray for this man's wife, that thou wouldst soften her heart in her rebellion and restore her to her husband and to you, through Jesus Christ, in whose name we pray, Amen."

This time the wounded soldier did not speak. The broken record had stopped playing as he struggled for a new thought. I had never seen someone who seemed so alone. All that he had known seemed contradictory. Even his clarity of thought, as he tried to sort it all out, to remember explanations, eluded him in that swirl of white around his head. He seemed fractured, pushed out of life, as though he was standing on its edge looking in to where he had once been a player. There were tears in his eyes when we left, his heart still breaking and his mind still fogging. Daddy had made some sort of contact through the mind's haze but now we too were leaving him. Our little circle of four broke up, and we walked down the stairs toward The Crusader.

The wounded soldier struggled to say, "Good-bye."

I sat in the truck with the window down, my arm burning on the heated metal, and looked down at the gravel flowing below us on our way down the drive back toward the yellow beige gates. Daddy's face was red in an intense mixture of sorrow and rage. Mother blew her nose in a white tissue. I knew the answers to this, I really did. It was the wife who had abandoned him when he was fighting for her freedom. How could she do that? How? I burst into a tirade of words against her. Daddy remained silent. As I looked over at him, my words were quieted by his powerlessness. If Daddy could not change this, then it could not be changed. Some things in life we are powerless against, like bullets in the night and other people's decisions to leave us. Both of those were now resident within the body of a boy standing at the foot of the hospital stairs. As we looked back at him in the side mirror as we drove away, he grew smaller and smaller. When he was out of sight, I headed back down the stairs to my internal fort, startled to find someone had spray painted on the wall—"I got a letter from my wife and she is leaving me for somebody back home." There was too much paint on the last word and it ran down in little rivulets.

After a silent trip through the streets of Saigon, we arrived home and I went down the ladder into the kitchen to get a soda out of the fridge. I pushed open the garage doors and pulled out a chair, scraping its legs on the uneven floor. Sitting at the little table, I tried to think. I tried to square the view of the world from behind the wheel of that new Chevy with the view from the bottom of those hospital steps looking right up into the face of a sniper's bullet. In one world Carmen was baking me cookies in the Pinecrest kitchen, in the other a wounded soldier was trembling and desperately holding onto a blue aeroform letter. I found I could not retain the focus of either view. My head seemed foggy, my mind wrapped in white. I could not sort out my thoughts. I could not find the right explanations. I could not stop the recorded memory of the wounded soldier spinning around in the kitchen playing and playing again.

God and the Gods

San Bruno, California

I was saved at age six. After a Sunday morning like so many others, Daddy and I were riding home together in the VW. Having my own personal theologian, I was beginning to apprehend the nature of man, the sinful separation from God, and the plan of redemption. Other kids' fathers may have coached them in little league; my coaching was in the intricacies of how the universe worked. Daddy coached in a gentle but persistent way. He helped me memorize Bible verses while we were rolling down the highway on vacation, saying, "Okay, Pal, here is how to remember it. It is eleven thirty at night, so you are up way past your bedtime. Out in the front lawn is a fruit tree, and you are hungry, and so you go out to pick some fruit, see? All right, let's hear it word-perfect this time."

Piece of cake, I thought. I cleared my throat and said forthrightly, "The fruit of the righteous is a tree of life, and he that winneth souls is wise, Proverbs 11:30."

Daddy encouraged, "That's my boy. You got the brains for this."

When I was a little older, he alliterated the five points of Calvinism for me while sitting in the parking lot of White Front waiting for Mother as she bought a new laundry basket.

On this particular Sunday, however, I was thinking about the story of the world and my place in it. God created it. Man disobeyed and became separated from God. God sent his only begotten Son to save us. If you believed, you had eternal life. If you did not, you went to hell! My problem was that I had not yet done anything particular about it. I sat up on the edge of the leatherette bucket seat, gripping the little handle above the glove compartment with both hands. I was feeling left out, separated from God, separated from Daddy, separated somehow from everybody. I wanted to find my place in the story. I wanted to ask him *that* question, but I was having a difficult time mustering some sort of courage. The trip lasted for blocks and blocks with endless red lights and slow cars puttering in front of us. Finally, as we were heading up Valley View Drive, right past Littleman's Supermarket, I blurted, "Daddy, how do you get saved?"

This was a question Mother and Daddy had been praying I would ask from the moment they learned of my presence in the womb. Daddy had been patient, though, and let each of his kids find their own way to the question.

"Well, Pal," he responded, "when we get home, let's go into the bedroom, and I'll show you right in your own Bible."

He was referring to my Children's Bible. It had a picture of Jesus on the front, his arms outstretched to a group of children, but the words in it were exactly like those in Daddy's thick black one with all the underlining. It was my first real Bible, and Carolyn had given it to me for Christmas just last month.

Sitting on the edge of their double bed, Daddy had me look up some verses in the book of Romans. It said, in words that I clearly understood, "If thou shalt confess with thy mouth the Lord Jesus, and shalt believe in thine heart that God raised him from the dead thou shalt be saved. For with the heart man believeth unto righteousness; and with the mouth confession is made unto salvation."

This was simple. I already believed it with all my heart; I just needed to confess it with my mouth. We knelt by the bed and prayed together, me following after his words, phrase by phrase: "Dear Jesus, I want you to be my Savior. I ask you to forgive me of my sins and come into my heart to live so that I can have eternal life with you."

I finished up with a sniff because this was an important moment, and I knew that we Peters sniffed at important moments. When we got up, Daddy reached into his coat pocket, took out his Mont Blanc fountain pen, and wrote the date in the margin of my Bible. Then I followed him down the hall to the living room. The rest of the family looked up at me when we came in, and Daddy said, "Do you have anything you want to say, Pal?"

I was mortified. They all already knew. I said quietly, "I asked Jesus into my heart."

Off and on over the next couple of years, Jesus living in our hearts was more than once the topic of discussion among the kids at church because most of us had not felt anything happen when it happened. Salvation did not happen just on the inside; it also happened on the outside. On the inside you had literally passed from death unto life, and Jesus had actually come to live in your heart. On the outside this was the moment when angels sang in heaven, when your name was written in the Lamb's Book of Life. But most of us did not feel anything or hear anything. Maybe we felt a little something, more responsible, more adult. But if you do not feel it, then how do you know it happened?

This question most often bubbled up into our conscious beings at revivals. Standing there, after an earnest sermon, one foot up on the crossbar of the chair in front of me and the hymn book balanced on its back, the power of the altar call was overwhelming. That gospel hymn "Just As I Am" could reach in and ever so gently hold my heart in its tune and words and whisper, "Danny, do you really believe? Are you really saved?" Revival preaching at its best was serious doctrinal exposition of Scripture—introduced by solos, illustrated by chalk talks, punctuated by anecdotes, finished off with an intense flourish, and followed by that sweet, sweet singing calling us to the arms of Jesus.

One particularly effective revival preacher got the whole junior department, boys and girls, to respond. The Holy Spirit swept through us like a wave, and our bodies and souls rode its crest down the aisle. That wave brought so many of us forward that we filled up the whole choir loft. After the service Daddy leaned on the choir director's podium and logically explained that we were already saved. Salvation was not something we could lose, but in our desire to be closer to the Lord we could rededicate our lives to witnessing at school and obeying our parents. Rededicating one's life to Jesus was a cleansing, an ordering. It was like setting up chairs in the sanctuary in a straight line, true to the lines running through the square tiles on the sanctuary floor. Life was sort of like those chairs: with use, the rows could get bendy and blurry, but a little adjustment would restore a sense of order to the whole sanctuary.

Through these times of intense devotion we learned that there was a distinct difference between trying to just look like a Christian and really acting like one. Looking like a Christian was just increasing our spiritual image in the eyes of others by show (like intentionally fraying the pages of your Bible to make it look well read). Really being a Christian was tougher. It was having a heart ablaze with Christ and a code of conduct that showed it. Periods of real commitment like this actually did change us, and we read our Bibles and prayed and witnessed and obeyed our parents. It gave us the energy to practice J.O.Y.—*J*esus first, *O*thers second, *Y*ourself last. It gave us the motivation to come to break-of-dawn prayer meetings, eat a donut, pray, and then be carpooled to school to invite our friends to that evening's service. This life was one of a relationship to God. If I felt out of sorts and blue some Sunday morning, wanting to stay at home and look out the picture window at the boats sailing in San Francisco Bay, Mother would never scold or talk about rules of behavior. She would simply say, "You are a Christian; you do whatever you think Jesus wants you to do." I went to church.

One Sunday night at the altar call I searched for and found the same sort of courage that I had needed to ask Daddy about getting saved. I turned around, carefully laid the hymn book on the seat, and walked down past all those straight rows of folding chairs to where Daddy stood. Daddy leaned down to me when I got to the front, and I whispered up into his ear, "I want to be baptized." At the end of that stanza he informed the congregation of my decision, and while we finished the last two stanzas of "The Old Rugged Cross," waiting to see if any one else had business to take care of with the Lord, I stood dwarfed beside him with my arm tightly wound around his pant leg.

A week later, at a quarter past six, I walked down the stairs into the waters and into Daddy's outstretched arms. I looked out to see what I could see, and I could not see anything except the riveted sheet metal lining on the inside of the baptistry wall. It was just me and Daddy and God in there together. We had practiced getting baptized at home the day before, so it was no big deal. I put both hands on his forearm, closed my eyes, and did not breathe. Daddy pronounced, "Danny Peters, upon your confession of faith I baptize you in the name of the Father, the Son, and the Holy Ghost. Amen." Then with the strength of those words and one arm he lowered me into the belly of Cedar Avenue Baptist Church. As I came up, the first thing I saw was water running off Daddy's forearm making dark streaks through the hair on the back of his hand. He patted me on the shoulder with that "well done, Pal" pat, and I sloshed up the stairs and into his study.

Daddy's study doubled as the men's dressing room and entrance to the baptistry (the kitchen did double duty for the women on the other side of the platform). Pulling the white robe off over my head, I looked down at my skinny body dripping in white cotton shorts that clung to my skin. Then it dawned on me. Daddy actually changed clothes in his study.

He had to be naked behind the study door while on the other side the congregation sang "There Is a Fountain." Here among the books, behind the desk, listening to those refrains, he dried his body. What did he think about when he was just a naked man? I know what he thought when clothed with the Word of God, but what about when he was just a naked man? I bent over and pulled my wet underwear off and looked down at my pencil with its small eraser tip. How he bore it I do not know. The privacy of body—so far removed from even any mention of existence—was so close to being public. Private only because humans can't see through walls. Yet this private thing had to be immersed in water in front of all those people. The body itself, not just the soul but the body. The thing I look down at while holding a hymn book, the thing in which Jesus and I live. It is his body that Daddy has to get wet and then dry off. Then he puts on his suit and speaks the Truth. The prophet of God. How did he make the transition from naked man to prophet of God, separated only by ten minutes and some plaster and wood? What would it have meant if he had been naked on the other side of the wall, on the singing and preaching side?

Leaving a puzzled puddle in front of his shelf of Old Testament commentaries, I went around the outside of the church, came in through the foyer, and sat in the back.

Saigon

When we first came to look at the house and they showed us upstairs, we were surprised that at the end of the long room stood a heavy black table with carved legs. On the table sepia photos of old people framed a small gold-colored Buddha. In front of the Buddha three joss sticks quietly twisted toward the open balcony doors. The pungent smell made the air in the room seem more dense than it already was, and the shadowy afternoon sun made broad paths through the smoke. Mr. Nguyen, knowing we were Christians and they were Buddhists, began in a polite voice, "This is our god room. We have a whole room dedicated to our ancestors, and we keep the incense always lit. We will move the god room to the other side of the house if you come live here."

"What exactly do you do in this room?" Daddy questioned.

"I am sorry, I do not understand," Mr. Nguyen said with a puzzled look on his face.

Daddy did not want to be rude to him or insult his religion; that was not the way to a person's soul. On the other hand, he wanted to clarify what went on in this room before he was ready to live in it, even if the incense and tables and pictures were removed. "I mean what do you do here in worship to your gods?"

Still puzzled by the question, Mr. Nguyen shrugged off its stupidity and simply said, "We pray."

That seemed to be okay with Daddy, and when we moved in, there was no sign of the gods. We did not think much about their gods until Phu came sheepishly up the steps just before Tet.

"Excuse me," he said in his most deferential tones, "My father wishes to know if we may celebrate Tet on the balcony to the old god-room."

"Well, I suppose so," Daddy answered. "Is there any special reason?"

"We think that when our gods come back this Tet maybe they will not be able to find us because we moved their room. We want to be in the same place as always so they do not get lost," Phu explained.

Daddy did not want to miss this opportunity to gently witness and said, "Are these gods powerful?"

"Oh yes," Phu answered, relieved that Daddy understood that one should not disappoint the gods.

"Phu, if they are so powerful, why will they get lost? Do you think that with all their power they will not be able to find the room on the other side of the house?" said Daddy planting a gospel seed.

"You do not wish to allow us to use the balcony Mr. Peters?" Phu asked.

"No, please go ahead. Just something to think about, that's all. Tell your father that it is our privilege and honor to have you use our balcony for your New Year."

Phu beamed, "Thank you. Thank you."

Daddy had been a little cautious about the gods of the pagans, but he also knew there were just as many superstitions. In fact, one of the challenges of our being here was trying to figure out the difference. What was of the devil and what was just superstition? Some missionaries chalked everything up to the devil, and we knew that the liberals believed only in superstitions. Daddy believed they were somehow different but connected.

"Pal," he would ponder, "what could make a villager who has lost everything, has no worldly possessions, no house, no job, and no land, sacrifice the only thing he has left, his water buffalo, the very thing that affords him the opportunity to farm rice and keep him alive?"

The only logical conclusion to Daddy's question was gods. Real gods. Culture and superstition just did not have that much power without something real behind it. Besides, the apostle Paul had clearly written that sacrifices given to idols were really sacrifices to demons. Maybe Daddy believed this because this is what we had done, sacrificed everything for the gospel, for God. If it was just cultural for the farmer, then maybe it would also be possible to be the same for us. Given that we had done this for our God, it was easy to understand the Vietnamese farmers doing it for their gods.

San Bruno

Daddy's beliefs about the reality of demons started when Mrs. Koltranian began coming to church last year. In San Bruno the ministry was about as normal as you could get. If a child wanted to be baptized, Daddy would take him out for an ice cream cone and talk to him about Jesus and his heart. If it was the first Tuesday night of the month it was the deacon's meeting. If it was fall it was the missions conference. Things were pretty predictable until Mrs. Koltranian came to church. She was from Somethingslavia and was heavy and peasantlike. She was also divorced and had a little boy. Most important, she was demon-possessed. One night she called Daddy and Mother to have them come pray with her. To Daddy's surprise, things got a bit out of control. As they were praying, a toaster flew across the room and hit the wall near where they were kneeling. This was when Daddy knew what he had long suspected—that Mrs. Koltranian was demon-possessed. He had even called Clyde Narramore, who told him it was a multiple-personality problem. Daddy considered this until household objects levitated when they prayed for her deliverance. After that demons were as material to Daddy as the toasters they threw. Fighting them took the power of God and all his angels because the demonic world was organized along military lines. The Bible clearly taught that there were different ranks under the chief Prince of Darkness. We appealed directly to the top on our side of the battle and the power of Jesus' shed blood, which had defeated Satan forever, even if the battle was temporarily still being waged.

The reality of demons permeated our church. When Harley and I found a cartoonlike tract in which demons had nightmares when Christians witnessed to the unsaved, we understood that evangelism was not only saving people's souls, it was a battle of good against evil. Through witnessing we could win the war against the invisible agents of Satan. We began an evangelistic club at church. We elected officers and collected offerings to buy hundreds of tracts. We mapped streets in San Bruno with red ink and then fanned out door to door, giving away tracts. Saturday mornings found us not on the ball field but trying to make literal the name of our gospel club—The Demons' Nightmares.

Saigon

It was the gospel that we were bringing to Vietnam, to the Vietnamese, to the communists, and to the GIs. Everybody needed it equally. So we preached and distributed hygiene packets and Gospels of St. John printed in either Vietnamese or English wherever we could. The most effective method was, of course, mass evangelism. The Crusader was a self-contained sound truck, so it could stop in a village and show a Laurel and Hardy movie to attract a big crowd. Then Daddy would preach and hand out Gospels. In the back of the Gospels was an offer of a free correspondence course, which a person could send for. Success was measured in terms of Gospels given out because "the Word of God would not return unto him void." If we did not have to round up a crowd on the street or in a village, all the better. Captive audiences were usually just that—Cheu Hoi camps offered us hundreds of captured or surrendered Viet Cong who came in from the heat, hungry and tired and defeated in spirit. ARVN basic-training camps offered other captive audiences, as did hospitals. In large part our mission was facilitated by the military: we went where they did, we did not go where they did not go.

If I was lucky, I could go with Daddy and Nang to the camps and help in the service.

"Pal, screw the aluminum base of the pole into the female fitting. I may need to tighten it myself. And then pull out four cases of Gospels and open 'em up. Use the knife in the glove compartment," Daddy ordered.

Using the bumper and fender to step up on and then
hopping past the windshield, I scrambled up the front of the
truck to the platform built on the top. Here we placed flood-
lights on the top of long poles and loudspeakers to blast 'em
with the Gospel.

"Daddy, let's turn up the amp so they can hear in the
back," I said with a question in my voice.

"They can hear, Pal. Besides we might get feedback and
distortion," he said.

"How does feedback work?" I asked. Big mistake. Daddy
talked about wavelengths and sound waves and distance to
mike from the direction of the amp while never breaking
stride sorting the wires and jacks into a pattern that would
carry the gospel. It took a couple of hours to get the whole
thing wired together, pull the cord on the Honda generator,
and light the area with the power of God.

One night in a Cheu Hoi camp I was not sure if I liked
being there all that much. As usual the camp commander had
the docile prisoners squat in long lines, twenty across and
twenty rows deep for the presentation. We had the tables piled
high with Gospels and hygiene packets to be handed out after
the service. This was similar to the preach-and-feed method
we used back in the rescue mission in San Francisco. After this
particular service so many men responded to the invitation to
know Jesus and meet with Daddy and Trang by the truck for
correspondence course instruction that we were suddenly surrounded by about fifty ex-Viet Cong. They pushed and
shoved to get closer, but Daddy's height allowed him to hand
out the papers over their heads. The press of the crowd and
the slow jostle of Vietnamese bodies and breath pushed me
away from Daddy and toward the back of the truck.

Faces were close to mine, eyes looking right into mine
and mouths smiling at me. I don't think they were especially
happy; they just seemed interested in me. Hands from the
crowd were reaching out and touching me, rubbing my arms,

patting me on the head, and stroking me. Daddy's usual radar was not picking up my frightened signals as he reached over the crowd of heads handing out Gospels. As they closed in around me, I felt trapped in my own white skin, conscious of its color and its texture, conscious that these men wanted to feel me.

Suddenly, a little panicked, I spun around and jimmied straight up the back of the truck to the platform on top, out of their reach. It was a place where I could look down at them from a safe place. The top of the truck was reserved for Daddy and Trang and me, and it gave me distance from them. Standing on the truck, breathing a little heavily, I heard Daddy call up, "You okay, Pal?"

"Fine," I called back.

The Cheu Hoi men were laughing and smiling, and one motioned for me to come down. I looked away, and stared though a cloud of moths to the buildings on the other side of the compound. I felt out of their physical reach, but I also felt trapped inside and very alone. The more I tried to ignore them, the more I felt isolated, cut off, as if they had pushed me onto the other side of an invisible wall, even cutting me off from myself. I stayed up there until the men were herded off to the barracks and then came down and silently helped disassemble the set-up.

Daddy did not find it strange that the men wanted to touch me. "Pal, some of them have never touched white skin before. They always want to feel the white hair on my arms. They can't believe it. We are so different from them that they are just curious about us," he said.

"I don't care. I don't like them rubbing me like that."

On the way home, my skin stayed distant from me, floating in space between who I was on the insides and my outside environment. It was like a wall, keeping me in and keeping them out. I was intensely aware of this other thing on my skin. Its whiteness. Brown hands stroked white, and I felt shaky. In a way they must have wanted to be white. Maybe, in a way I did not understand, they wanted my flesh.

If I was white, Phu was very brown. His skin absolutely shone in the Mekong sun as though it had been polished like the brass Buddha on the god table. Thongs, shorts, and a floppy shirt covered his body with the easy rhythm of the breeze as we roamed around the factory or walked over to the riverbank. I wore leather sandals like his, but I never ventured out without clean white crew socks, preferably with two blue stripes around the top, stretched halfway up my calf. Plaid Bermuda shorts and a short-sleeve oxford button-down shirt completed my daily wardrobe.

Near the river, Phu, Huong, and I squatted and poked and pried and talked and laughed. One afternoon, when we had more time than usual because Phu had less homework than usual, we all felt more free, more easy, able to enjoy an unexpected hour of vacation. There was a war, yes, but we were on the right side, and we were winning. There would be a cost to some, but principles were just that, principles. Phu and Huong were going to join the Vietnamese Air Force, following in the steps of their older brother. Sitting on the riverbank, Phu looked out over the slow pulse of the waters and said, "I will be a pilot. I will fight."

With a sharp sweep of his hand he showed us the line of his flight. He continued in his best English: "Technology and honor meet in the fighter jet. Built for speed and maneuverability, it is the most precise and effective way to protect our land." As I listened to him speak, it was our first moment of knowing one another as men. I saw the world as an adult. No longer pretending to play war in the eucalyptus trees with the Pinecrest gang, I knew that the time was coming to be men, to fight for ourselves and for this land. Perhaps I would volunteer—I could speak a little Vietnamese. I could be very helpful; I understood what this war was about and did not doubt my capability in helping to finish it.

Phu stopped short and looked at me, "What do you do in America on a day like today?" he asked.

Hmm, I thought, "Oh yeah," I suddenly remembered. "We'd play baseball."

"Baseball? I've heard of that," quipped Huong. "How do you play it?"

"Come on, I'll show you."

I jumped up and looked around for an open flat space. The island was perfect. We crossed the bridge single file, and I started to look for a stick and some rocks. Finding a branch and some pebbles, I showed them how to swing and hit. While they whiffed frantically, I began to lay out the base paths from home to first to second to third. Phu and Huong were laughing themselves sick trying to hit the rocks. Occasionally I would hear a "kwruk," and they would yell excitedly, "I did it! I did it!"

I was dragging my foot behind me in a wavy line between third and home base when I heard a high-pitched whissing sound over my head. It was loud enough to command all of our attention. Then again. And quickly again. We looked up and around. From the other side of the island, on the far bank of the river, we saw puffs of smoke and heard the pop of guns and then whizzes above our heads. We were puzzled for about three seconds, and then it instantly dawned on us, and we all hit the dirt. We were getting shot at! Near the bridge, closer to our side of the river, the MPs began to return fire across the island to the far side. We lay in the sand, its tiny grit sifting into our hair, and listened to the bullets' efficient sound above.

"Are we in crossfire?" I whispered tensely.

"I don't know," Phu said. "Maybe they are shooting at us!"

Crawling facedown on our bellies, we inched our way back toward the bridge. With every scoot a puff of red dirt blew up into a little cloud around our heads. We did not wait for it to settle but kept going as fast as we could, creating a little stream of dust behind us. The whizzing bullets were intermittent. One, two, three. Then nothing. Then one, two more. We split the last stalks of grass just above the embankment that cut down to the planks that could carry us across the river and back to safety. Waddling like ducks, we slid down the embankment until we hit the bridge.

Pent-up energy was suddenly released when Huong yelled, "RUN!"

Instantly we sprinted for our lives, the pop pop pop behind us now. The sound faded as we ran straight down the lane toward the main factory building near the house.

Out of breath and panting, we leaned against the warm tin siding and waited for the fire in our lungs to cool. Then without a word we slung our arms around each other and walked three abreast. Friends. American and Vietnamese, in peace or in war. The earlier dreams of fighting had evaporated as quickly as the possibility of a lazy afternoon baseball game.

Arm in arm we walked quietly back to the house, repeating all the details of how close each whizzing bullet had been to the very ear that heard it. Daddy was unloading Gospels from the truck when we ambled through the gate and entered the yard. The look of concern on his face was obvious as all three of us took part in telling the story.

The next day Daddy asked to talk to me.

"Pal," he said rather embarrassedly, "uh, it's not good to walk like you did with Phu and Huong yesterday."

"Walk like what?"

"Well, to, uh, to walk with your arms around each other. It's just not good for boys to be holding hands and to walk arm in arm."

"Really? Why?"

"It just isn't done. It's not good. I do not want you to walk that way anymore."

"Okay," I shrugged. There was no explanation but I could tell from Daddy's voice that this was a *very* serious thing. This was in the same category as not calling Todd's dad Father, even if he was a priest ("We have only one father, Pal, and he is in heaven," Daddy had once sternly corrected my reference to Todd's dad).

That day I faced the task of telling Phu and Huong we couldn't hold hands or walk that way anymore.

Phu felt very bad when I told him. He thought that it must be against our religion.

"I am sorry if we offended your religion, your god. We will not do that anymore. In Vietnam our gods do not mind, and we like to be good friends."

Phu's vision of my god was about as clear as my visions of his. This had first become clear over a discussion as to why he always won at chess and I always won at Stratego. He finally summed it up with a light in his face that showed true illumination: "Your god likes Stratego and our god likes Chess!"

Con Đường Gồ Ghề (Sỏi Đá)

8
Rocky Road

Saigon

Some things were the same here, like Daddy driving, and some things were different here, like Daddy driving. The sometimes dust and sometimes mud road leading into our house was walled along both sides by those omnipresent pale yellow concrete slabs. A temple roof rose above the wall running down the right-hand side, and the wall on the left propped up against its back a collection of little huts and tin sheds. A Saigon suburb. Daddy drove carefully between these walls, The Crusader barely squeezing through as it lurched into a rut, first right, then left, its wide mirrors perilously close to being scraped clean off. He drove hulked over the steering wheel, grinding the gears and soaking his J.C. Penney dress shirt with the concentration of trying to steer a two-ton Chevy truck down a lane built for a bicycle. These kinds of driving conditions meant that we didn't go anywhere on the spur of the moment. Driving here was carefully planned to account for darkness, time, traffic, and safety. Back home driving was much more spontaneous.

San Bruno

We didn't have many family traditions other than our schedule controlled by the weekly and yearly cycles of church—Sundays and Wednesdays, Christmas, Easter, and the annual missions conference. But we did have one tradition that defined us as a family, probably because it was Daddy's only vice of the flesh—ice cream. In the evening, people noises filled our house: Carolyn arranged choir music on the piano, Carmen listened to Johnny Mathis records, Conrad talked on the phone, Mother sewed in the hallway, and Daddy squeaked in the rocker reading a theological tome. Sitting upside down on the couch, one leg swung over the arm, the other over the back, I observed the family from my bottommost position.

Tonight boredom ruled and kept me from pestering the whole family to the borders of their sanity. On another night, Daddy, his face red from laughter at my antics, protestations, and impersonations, gave in to the complaints of Conrad (who feigned concentration on homework at the dining room table) and sent me to the basement to sit on the washing machine. When I could be quiet for five whole minutes, I could return. Until then I had to stay down there so the adults could get some work done. I sat there for a minute straining to keep quiet, repeatedly bursting out in laughter as I tried to pass the time. Finally, my insides feeling tenuously settled I headed up the stairs and opened the door. Peering around to check on the family condition, we all burst into laughter, and Daddy pointed me back to the basement. Some nights, though, like tonight, boredom arrived and overstayed its welcome, like that old windbag who sat in the living room just last week complaining about the color of paint in the Sunday school rooms.

After Carmen got done mooning over her music and moved to the dining room table to roll her hair, Daddy put on his favorite record, "The Worlds Greatest Overtures." This was my favorite record as well because of the live cannon booms on "1812." After exhausting myself by directing an imaginary orchestra in front of the living room mirror, I resumed my upside-down position on the couch. Hanging my head backward off the couch I began my strategy.

"It sure is hot in here tonight," I started.

No response.

"Boy, chocolate ice cream sure would taste good. Do we have any ice cream left?" I asked light-heartedly, being careful to use my high-but-not-too-whiny voice.

No response except the whir of Mother's sewing machine.

Finally Conrad chimed in from inside the icebox door, "What happened to the rest of the Rocky Road?" Nobody said anything, but I noticed Daddy smile slightly behind his book.

"Let's go get some ice cream," I began encouraging. "Come on, it's eight-thirty and Littleman's closes at nine."

Daddy sympathized in an exhale of words, "Aaugh, Pal, I am too tired to go out again. Maybe Conrad will take you." (He said this because Conrad had learned to drive recently enough that the family was still getting free errands out of him.)

"Connie, come on, let's go," I chirped as I rolled off the couch into a backwards somersault onto the floor. "Let's just hop in the VW and go-o-o-o! Please ... please," I danced.

"Go where?" Conrad kidded in his usual avoidance of a direct question.

Knowing that the centrifugal force of this conversation was soon to cast us out of that boredom and right into Littleman's, I ran down the hall, hurdled a pile of Mother's fabric and patterns, broke left at the bend, and slid through the bedroom door to get my new S.F. Giants windbreaker.

We always bought chocolate. That was our moral duty as Peters. If we broke down and got some weenie flavor for Mother, like cherry vanilla or butter brickle, we would supplement it with a can of Hershey's syrup. We had ritualized the process of getting every drop out of a Hershey's can. First, there was the pouring stage, when it came out the triangled hole in the top in a thick, black flow. Second, there was the stage when, after it was half gone and had been sitting in the ice box, we would put the can on the electric stove burner and warm it up till a thin line ran out in little squigglies over each mound of ice cream. Finally, there was the can-opener stage. This was scraping the bottom of the barrel. Squeezing the long handles of the can opener till your knuckles turned red and turning the little crank carefully, one could liberate the rest of the chocolate. After removing the whole lid, we would spoon out the sticky sides and bottom, not forgetting the underside of the top, even though that could be white with fuzz if someone left the can out on the counter too many times. It was over bowls of ice cream that Daddy's tie came off and we planned church events; scheduled rides for the next day; discussed school, friends, keeping our rooms clean, and where we would probably not go on vacation.

Saigon

Arriving in Saigon, we bought two things at the PX almost immediately. First was a flashlight so we could have light at night—something I did not think about at the time. Daddy bought a big gray lantern with one of those heavy square batteries. Second was a beige and chrome GE transistor radio so he could keep up with the news on Armed Forces Radio. It was to the PX we went to get these kind of things.

Heading into the PX, we walked past a row of men urinating on one of the yellowed walls just around the corner from the front gate. As we passed, one of the men turned his head and, bending it sideways and down from the neck, blew his nose. Out came a long green string that swung like a wet rubber band. Then, with another short blast, it fell into the dirt near our feet. Mother was her usual poised self and just kept walking with Daddy, her legs needing two steps to keep up with every one of Daddy's. Rounding the corner, we were confronted by a group of boys who rushed up and danced close around us, gesturing intensely toward the street and shouting, "Bad cowboy, bad cowboy." After some moments of exchange, we finally understood the deal. For one hundred piasters they would watch our truck and yell for help if it was getting robbed. Having been a street-wise kid in New York with a fine-tuned Calvinist understanding of human nature, Daddy figured that they were probably not going to protect the truck—but if you did not pay them they probably would go *get* a bad cowboy and then watch for *our* return while he broke into it.

The truck would have been a gold mine too. It had a gas generator, microphones, amplifiers, projectors, lights, and all sorts of wires and jacks that we hooked together to run evangelistic meetings in villages, street fairs, and military camps. Daddy had invented an alarm system, hooking all the doors to the horn with clear nylon line since it would be hard to see at night as it crisscrossed the cab from door handles to switches under the dash. Every morning, I carefully crawled through the double back doors, and unhooked the system before he drove me to school. Unfortunately, this system was too complicated to hook up more than once a day. So, we paid the hundred piasters and went into the PX to the happy shouts of "Good cowboy, good cowboy."

The PX aisles reminded me of Littleman's: lots of canned food, soda pop, and a long white freezer with ice cream. After picking up the essentials that we had come for—razor blades, Vitalis, batteries, and canned tuna—Daddy and I wound our way back to the ice cream and lingered over the freezer, enjoying the cold hovering air while picking out a flavor. Back and forth we went, considering any flavor that had the required degree of chocolate resident in it somewhere.

"How does chocolate chip sound, Pal?" Daddy asked.

"Marble fudge looks pretty good," I said.

"There is always good ol' chocolate," he countered.

"I dunno. I think the Rocky Road," I finally concluded.

Daddy fished around in the bottom of the case looking for one that was frozen really hard. After tossing a few boxes around, he found one that he thunked with his finger, and found, to his immense satisfaction, that it was as solid as a rock. Even so, since they came only in a half-gallon size and we could not get it home before it melted, it presented us with a sticky problem. We could not pass up the ice cream, though, so we decided that the three of us would eat the whole thing while we sat in the truck.

Walking back to the truck, I flexed my almost-existent preadolescent muscles by volunteering to carry the case of soda pop. Daddy carried the bag with the thing foremost on our minds—Rocky Road ice cream. Luckily the wetting wall was empty, although a sweet smelling cloud remained. We were almost to the truck when the same gang of street orphans reappeared. This time they said in broken English, "No bad cowboy, no bad cowboy," signaling our truck was safe and holding their hands out for another tip. But our hands were busy carrying things beyond their imagination and probably beyond their caloric intake of a whole week. Somehow they seemed to know this.

The shouting turned to pleas and cajoling smiles, then to darker words and close clutching hands. They followed us as close as they dared, which was too close for comfort as Mother and I gathered in a little tighter to Daddy. The shadow of Daddy's dimensions kept them at bay, and I was relieved to see that he was having the same success giving them "the look" that I myself was familiar with in certain circumstances of borderline behavior. We unlocked the back doors of the truck and stashed the bags and the pop. Going up through the inside of the truck I opened the front doors, and Mother and Daddy got in. Locking the doors behind us, we sat in the hot moist interior of the truck, trying to decide what to do about the crowd of kids outside. We decided the best thing to do was to ignore them and they would go away, which, after a few minutes seemed to come true.

Once we were alone, I rolled down the window for air. Mother rifled through the glove compartment and came up with a couple of spoons and a handful of Kleenex. Mother and Daddy shared one spoon and I got the other. Sitting three across, we scooped out big bites of the quickly softening ice cream. I pulled out big hunks and rounded off the tops as I drew each and every spoonful back out of my mouth, my knuckles tipped with chocolate from the sides of the carton. Daddy sighed in the pure cold pleasure of it and said, "Boy, this hits the spot, doesn't it!"

My mouth was too full to answer.

We were about halfway into the carton when one of the street orphans circled the truck and saw the ice cream. He rushed up to my door and grabbed the handle with both hands. I turned to him and through those brown eyes our souls locked in an instant of recognition that would never leave me. His face not six inches away from me, I saw my reflection in his eyes. Within his flesh resided an opposite world—violence, starvation, meanness, aloneness. It was a world that in that moment I somehow entered or, like some cultural poltergeist, entered me. A world of another little boy's dreams and hungers. We were just two kids—except he was starving, and I was gulping Rocky Road ice cream.

The instant passed and quickly replaced itself by the fear of being overtaken by the crowd. I cranked up the window, leaving him to knock on the outside and cry, "Please, good cowboy, please, good cowboy, please, please." Immediately five or six faces on each side of the truck peered in, little brown hands clutching at the door handles, knocking on the windows. The street orphans jumped up and down trying to get a look at the white boy eating ice cream.

Mother, Daddy and, I looked at each other in a pause of hesitation. We couldn't eat it all anyway, so I took one last scoop, and handed the carton to Daddy. In silent agreement he rolled down the window about three inches, just enough to crush the carton out, and then watched it disappear into a swarm of bodies on the ground. They piled on top of each other and shouted and pulled at each other's hair and clothes trying to get a mouthful. The groveling, grunting bodies were mostly those of the bigger boys, the littlest ones keeping their distance, knowing enough to just lean against a tree and watch.

Daddy twisted the key, and The Crusader turned over and started with its usual reliability, but we could not back up until the boys were done, so we sat there idling as they finished off the ice cream. It took only a few minutes. As they finished, an M.P. jeep pulled up to a stop sign down at the corner. "Good cowboy, good cowboy," they yelled hopefully as they ran toward the GIs.

My body rocked with the motion of the truck as Daddy maneuvered it back and forth, cranking on the steering wheel, putting it in second gear and then into reverse as he tried to maneuver it out of our tight parking spot. I felt stunned and self-conscious. My body was sitting here in the truck, its mouth still ice-cream cold, but I was no longer inside of it and I could no longer taste the Rocky Road in my mouth. I began to feel sick to my stomach, the first time I ever felt sick from eating Rocky Road. I concentrated on keeping the Rocky Road in my stomach, where it would be ice cream eaten, and out of my throat, where it would be evil vomited. Eating that ice cream in front of those kids put me into a relationship with them in a new way that I did not understand. A relationship between that kid and me with ice cream on my upper lip. Me on the inside and him on the out.

9
Saigon Christmas

Saigon

We sat in straight-backed chairs arranged in a circle, sipping tea and eating cookies we had bought at the PX. Mother did no Christmas cooking this year because we had no oven. We made a trip to the PX instead and bought some cookies in a round blue tin, some tinsel, a little package of bulbs, and a tiny fake tree. One package of bulbs was enough to cover it. We finished it off with the little strands of tinsel and set it on a table in the corner. To celebrate Christmas we invited Trang and Pastor and Mrs. Loi over for tea and cookies. Mrs. Loi sat deferentially with her hands folded and her head quick to nod in assent. Trang translated for her the important things. This was the American holiday. The Vietnamese holiday, Tet, would be coming in about five weeks.

I had on a new shirt that Conrad sent me for Christmas and was feeling sharp all dressed up in my holiday best. I felt large in the presence of Mrs. Loi, whom even I dwarfed. I usually felt small next to Daddy's frame house of a body, but the frail Mrs. Loi, weighing perhaps seventy pounds, made me feel so large that I became clumsy. My foot clunked on my knee as I crossed my legs. My elbow poked at the arm of the chair. I was concentrating on balancing my plate of cookies and holding my tea when Pastor Loi turned and addressed me directly.

I looked up and straight into his kind eyes. He gently asked,

"Do you miss being at home for Christmas?"

There it was, the unaddressed question of homesickness, the unmentioned feelings.

"Yes," I nodded.

"Do you miss getting so many presents?"

He had looked beyond me and seen the little tree barren of presents underneath and cared about me.

"Yes," I lied. I lied because I was getting presents. Even if it wasn't going to be a San Bruno haul, I would receive more than all his children combined. Daddy had wanted to avoid looking rich in front of the national pastors, so he had hidden all the presents under the bed and instructed me not to mention them.

San Bruno

Christmas was the pinnacle of the year. From Christmas the year swung downward in a gentle arc, interrupted by the opening of Spring Training and the high hopes for another shot at the Yankees in the World Series, then the end of the school year with the first breeze of summer blowing across the school yard. Once school began again, it was a long haul, but Christmas was coming. The best part of Christmas was not Christmas morning nor the Christmas cantata at church. The best part of Christmas was any one of those lucky nights when, for unknown reasons, I found myself alone in the living room. I turned out the lamp at each end of the couch, crossed the room to turn off Daddy's gooseneck reading lamp behind the gray rocker, then in one half-back motion spun around and plunked down in it. I curled both feet up under me, scrunched my shoulders into its rippled back, and slipped quietly over the rim of the world into Christmastree Land, blurry and multicolored.

We were traditional, Douglas firs every year. They were the cheapest, just one more thing preacher families had to deal with. We couldn't have a more showy tree than other people in the church. Flashy trees, uniform on both sides, flocked and flood lit, were for the bankers and executives in the church. Plain Douglas firs, modestly decorated, were best for the preacher. One nice couple in the church gave us a huge but ever-so-gaudy Christmas tree bulb, which Mother did not like but was obligated to hang prominently every year, sacrificing a whole branch in the effort.

As I rocked in the rocker, the darkness of the room was pierced by four dozen spots of color. The tree glowed in red and yellow and blue and green in random but even spacing all over the tree. Getting them right was left to Mother's discretion and Daddy's reach. Unpacking the lights always produced a jumbled set of black wires with pointy bulbs, some glazed with hardened remnants of white foam. Conrad and Daddy were the electrical men, the bulb men. They sat and untangled long lines of bulbs from one end of the living room to the other.

"Danny, move that second string there to the left to make more room."

Tip-toeing across the strands, being very careful to not step on any, I squatted and said with my usual hesitancy about things mechanical, "This one?"

"Yeah, pull that one over toward Carolyn's foot. Carolyn, don't move your foot without looking now."

"What now?" I asked.

"Pal, come down here behind me and plug this one in and let's see if we have anything," Daddy instructed.

"Nope."

"Fiddlesticks!" he exclaimed.

"You know what to do, Pal?" he asked.

"Sure, just go down the line and tighten every bulb." I answered.

"Right, and if that doesn't work, then we will start replacing the bulbs one by one to see which one is burned out. Conrad has the bag of spare bulbs by him."

Daddy stood up to stretch his back, and we all heard the quick crunch of a one-inch light bulb under two hundred pounds of righteousness.

Conrad laughed and said, "I know what's wrong with that string!"

Mother relegated me and my stocking feet to the couch to wait out the clean-up while she went after the vacuum.

Now, in the solitude of darkness I rocked slowly and looked at the double bank of lights—the tree reflected in the picture window giving me two trees. Behind the tree, through the picture window, the particularity of winter on the Bay reflected quickly appearing and then dissolving lights, each one floating just under the surface of the water. Lights of jet airplanes landing at the airport, lights from Oakland, lights from a boat anchored south of Candlestick. I was encased in lights, very small and each one colored. It was a time when I didn't mind if my glasses were broken again. Sometimes, even if they weren't, I took them off so the lights fuzzied and lived together, just like we did.

Saigon

Hearing "I'll Be Home for Christmas" on Armed Forces Radio, and knowing I would not, brought a crash of emotions. Propped up like too much junk behind a closet door, my emotions were barely crammed in. I had been mostly successful up to now about being happy about Christmas. Happiness was the cornerstone of our family often expressed in Daddy's injunction at the first sign of a pout: "Get happy, Pal!" Happiness was also the foundation of our faith, sure testimony to a surrendered life lived in the center of God's will. Outside of God's will one was miserable. Saigon at Christmas was God's will for me, and I was happy. But the music made it hard. It opened that closet door, and all that junk tumbled out onto the floor of my holiday. How could I pretend that Christmas would be okay in Saigon? Daddy and Mother knew it wasn't really the same here for Christmas—but people were dying without the Lord; so couldn't we find it in us to make that sacrifice, to lose a Christmas, for these people?

"Isn't that really what Christmas is all about Pal?" he asked. "Couldn't this be a *real* Christmas?"

Every year Daddy toyed with the idea of foregoing Christmas and sending our money to the mission field, only to be talked out of it by the rest of us. This year he got his wish, no commercialism clouding the joy of giving the ultimate gift, yourself. Mother was lonely, but she bore it with a teared eye, her quiet strength restraining her loneliness to keep it from burdening Daddy and the ministry.

We kept our chins up until Christmas Eve. Lined up three across in the pew at the International Church for Christmas Eve service, we were singing "The Birthday of the King," when I lost control of my chin. I looked straight ahead and tried to hold the spasms in my stomach from becoming sobs. It silently spread to Mother, who handed her half of the hymn book to Daddy and began vigorously rubbing her nose with a hanky. Daddy stood straight, his own voice stifled to silence. He looked down at the floor as the music continued around us. It wouldn't be so bad if I didn't have the best family in the world, the best brother, the best sisters, the closest, most loving family I had ever seen. No burying my head in Aunt Esther's soft bosom thanking her for that special present, no laughter from the kitchen as Conrad and Carmen played another game of "gotcha last," staying just this side of irritation, no shopping for Carolyn's cologne or Momoo's broach. Fractured by The Call. Compound. Through the skin. Bone poking out. Marrow draining.

I longed for and dreaded hearing that punch line over the little transistor radio—"if only in my dreams." It was here I learned the preciousness of memory, unlike the GI at the hospital whose memory was garbled and out of focus, my mind was a place in which I could live. It brought safety. Music carried me far away. It drew me home. I floated over the Pacific, making it as far as Guam or Hawaii, but never far enough to make it home for Christmas. I couldn't encompass the distance, but I could sit and watch from afar a star in the sky that twinkled its love over San Bruno. Would they know that the star in the sky, the one that caught Carmen's attention as she left church, was me? Trying to shine my light on home. Trying to rise in the East and set in the West.

Con Son Island

The Littletons invited us to spend the week between Christmas and New Year's with them on Con Son Island. Mrs. Littleton knew Colonel Ky's wife from a women's Bible study and had accepted the invitation to use the Kys' vacation house on Con Son Island. The U.S. Coast Guard had a base there, and there was a prison on the island, but it was considered safe. Safe from the war. We met the Littletons at Tan Son Nhut Airport. Bags and boxes, children and the maid waited on the tarmac to board the C–130.

The plane vibrated by direct nerve through the metal bench as I strapped myself in. Daddy was as relaxed as he could be, knowing that he was going to have to spend this much time with another family and try to get to the bathroom to shave or whatever without being noticed. His privacy was protected by a Jericho-like wall that could be blown down only by occasional surprises, like the time I brought Dougie Hampshire into the house one afternoon and found Daddy asleep on the couch. He muttered for us to play outside. Later he told me to not bring anybody in the house if he needed to sleep in the daytime.

The C–130 lifted off, and soon the patchwork of the Mekong gave way to a line of blue stretching out before us. The very blueness of it washed out the grit in my eyes and cleaned out the clutter of land, just as the Pacific had always done. On board we explored as far as we could and, best of all, talked to the pilots and co-pilots. One of them asked me if I wanted to navigate the landing. He picked me up and plopped me in a chair that dangled from the ceiling so that my feet swung freely in the cavernous abdomen of the plane. I looked at the green dials and lights. These were the instruments one needed to navigate. They provided the information needed to fly in the dark. I couldn't read them. I sat in mid-air, facing the instruments, unable to navigate. Someone else piloting my life over the ocean and beyond.

Con Son was white sand everywhere. A truck came up to the plane on the runway, and we all piled in and rumbled over to the other side of the island. The first task was to get water into the tank for household use. Mr. Littleton talked to the truck driver and ordered water. The Littleton kids and I burst into the house, looked in every room, dropped our bags on the floor, and ran out to the lip of the South China Sea. It was too blue. The contrast of colors was so primary it struck me in the eyeballs and almost jerked my head back. It was harsh in beauty, different from the muted blue and gray shades of fog where the Pacific rolled into Half Moon Bay or the browns and greens in the haze of Saigon. These colors seemed more vivid than life itself.

Looking back at the house, I saw a large cart lumbering up the road, pulled by a water buffalo with loose skin. It was the water man. When he arrived at the house, he straddled the cart, swinging big buckets of water out of the back of the cart and up and into the tank, talking with the Littletons' maid.

"Come on," I shouted, "Let's go look at the water buffalo."

The four of us ran drunkenly through the sand toward the big brown animal. Out of respect for its enormity we approached with caution. It stood there, in Daddy's words, a "beast." Its tail swatted the flies on its back, and it blinked a bored eye as it waited for the next command that would drive it down the road, not much closer to the end of another day. We stood and looked at it for awhile, not saying much, then went inside.

If this really was the vacation house of Colonel Nguyen Cao Ky, the vice-president and former premier of South Vietnam, it was nothing to brag about. It was a bamboo hut with a large central room and six smaller rooms opening off to the side. There was no indoor plumbing, so the bathroom was pretty much an indoor outhouse. There was a ceramic toilet over a hole in the ground near the back of the house, complemented by a nice roll of American toilet paper mounted on the wall. Between the wall and the toilet was a big wicker basket into which you tossed the paper after wiping. Someone, not me, emptied it occasionally. Water came from the concrete tank filled by Water Buffalo Man. For light there was a bare electric bulb hanging in the middle of each room. In the central room the bulb hung over a long picnic table where we congregated in the semidarkness. It was too dim for Daddy, so he rummaged around in the cook's boxes and found some tin foil. Cutting it and creasing the seams together, he made a reflector so the light would at least come down and not be lost upon the geckos in the thatch, who did not have important books to read.

By the second night the rhythm of the vacation was set. Morning strolls on the beach. Explorations of blue and white. Food together at the table. A field trip to see a papaya plantation. Dinner. Then with great anticipation we waited for night when we would patter down to the ocean, hearing its stillness, and approach with respect. Then at a whispered signal we would all turn on our flashlights and sweep them across the creamy grit in a wide arc to spot crabs skittering sideways in surprise and indignation. The first one to see a crab would shout, "I see veecee, I see veecee." Then out with the lights to await the next brave crabs to beach and be caught in the light.

Stan and Nora found the first two and broke into the victory chant, "I see veecee, I see veecee." On the third flash of light I discovered the first crab speeding back to the foam and cried, "I see veecee, I see veecee." Daddy was standing near me so he could also see and appreciate my victory. Just as my heart crested like a gentle Con Son wave of joy, Daddy uttered a low-toned and even rebuke that only I could hear. "Pal!" he said. It was all that needed to be said. I knew that I had transgressed some way of being Christian and had dulled our testimony of all that it meant to shine as a light for Christ, although I wasn't sure how. I didn't ask. After that, if I was lucky enough to spot a crab, I said, "There's one! There's one!"

After crabbing on the beach, we headed back to the hut, the yellow light under the aluminum foil making each window a dull and hallowed home. We sat around for a moment recounting crab stories before heading off to bed. More of the same tomorrow.

Mother and Daddy and I didn't sleep together in the same bed here as we did in Saigon, because our room was furnished with three single beds that looked like remnants from old army barracks. Aside from the beds and a brown straight-backed chair, the room was barren. The gray cement floor was unstained. Yellow and brown bamboo poles rippled up and down the walls. The dominant color was provided by three stark white mosquito nets on the beds. I climbed in, still a little blue from being caught yelling "I see veecee." Feeling quiet, I tucked the netting in around the mattress and spent a minute killing a couple mosquitoes that were on the inside before they killed me. Then Daddy pulled the string, and soon I was alone with his snore and the sound of the South China Sea.

I lay draped in the white of the mosquito net, the sea oozing in through its open mesh. Shrugging my shoulders sideways and wiggling my butt down, I created an indentation in the mattress and settled into myself for the night. The absence of the bombing was palpable, a counterpoint of peace that robbed the night of tranquillity. Even in its absence the war was present. But an element of fear was gone, dulled, drifted out to an island on the horizon, awaiting its return, with ours, to Saigon. I exhaled a deep breath and slept.

Screaming tore through the blackness, white as the mosquito net. I twisted violently upward into the net, invisible to my eye but present on my face. The shrill of the scream was so close that it vibrated in my body, and I wasn't sure if it was me screaming or not. Commotion flooded the house, hysterical screaming in Vietnamese, banging wooden things, furniture scraping, and people fumbling for lights to the calls of "What is it?" "Are you all right?"

Daddy was out of the bed and across the room before I could get myself disentangled from my cocoon. He threw open the door of our bedroom and yanked the light string above the table in the common room. It lit and swung wildly, throwing monstrous shadows across the wall, racing up my face and then departing to leave me in darkness before swinging back and illumining me for a moment once again.

Mr. and Mrs. Littleton ran to the back of the house where the hysterical screaming continued. "It's the maid," Daddy said as he turned back into the room to talk to Mother. I could see Mother's shadowed form. She was sitting up in her bed, leaning on one elbow with one knee drawn up close to her chin.

"Johnny," she whispered, "what do you think is the matter?"

"I don't know."

The Littletons' maid was no longer screaming, but I could still hear the muffled sobs and the tonal melodies of Vietnamese as the conversation proceeded. Eventually Daddy encroached to the edge of the back room where the maid slept, leaving Mother and me to wonder. I took the opportunity to kick out the sheets and slip out under the net. I headed to the doorway to look toward the back. The shadows had grown quiet and even, bending and flowing over the concrete floor and wooden table, giving the room a museum appearance.

Daddy returned with a grim look on his face. His eyes were hard and set against the night. On guard. Uneasy.

"What happened?" I whispered.

"Uh, there was an intruder who tried to get into her bed with her."

"What?"

"She woke up when some guy tried to lie down beside her."

"Who? Why would anybody do that?"

"Well, uh, he wanted to kiss her."

"Somebody broke into the house in the middle of the night just to kiss the maid?"

"I guess."

"Why?"

"Well, because of lust."

"Lust?"

"Inordinate desire," Daddy explained. "When you want something too much."

"Oh, brother!" I exclaimed, knowing Daddy had revealed all that he was going to about the intruder and the maid. The rest was a mystery.

The next day the Littleton kids and I circled the house looking for clues. All we could conclude was that the sound of banging wood that we had heard was the shutters above the indoor toilet being thrown open as the man dived out. He must have taken a running leap, stepped on the toilet, and hurled himself through the window. That room smelled so bad we had left it open for the night. To let our stench out, we let the intruder in.

Mrs. Littleton was sure it was Water Buffalo Man come back because he and the maid had spent a long time conversing that afternoon and had even discussed which villages they came from and exchanged family information. "This is a sign of advanced courting and intimacy in Vietnam," she explained. "He evidently thought that she was giving him an invitation to . . . to kiss her."

Con Son's peace and good tidings were gone, and we all remained edgy that day. The maid was afraid and stayed in the house. We played by the sea and built sand castles in the sand. That night we locked up the whole house, including the stinking bathroom's window, and went to bed bombarded by an uneasy anticipation of the darknesses of Vietnam. I lay down and scrunched myself into the bed. Here there were no twinkling lights on the Bay and no reflections of past Christmases in the picture window, just the deformed shadows of a yellow bulb giving way to blackness.

10
Roadblock

Preparations for Tet began a few days ago, the women and maids of Phu's family making preparations in the kitchen while Phu and Huong worked around the house. Missionary veterans prepared us with some of the rules. First, make sure you are not the first guest to arrive at any Vietnamese household. It was customary to visit special friends, but it was too big a risk to be the first. The luck of the following year for the whole family, good or bad, was determined by the first visitor. We sure did not want to be blamed for bad luck and thus diminish the gospel message. Second, be sure to give a little money to the children in a red envelope. Third, be sure to present it politely with both hands, indicating that it is a special gift.

Tet eve began much like an American New Year's Eve with firecrackers, pot banging, and much merriment. Phu's family hung up lights and lanterns in the garden and waited till exactly midnight to light the long string of firecrackers. It hung five feet long off our balcony railing and twisted, jerked, and blasted in yellow pops. The next morning we would go through the pile of red paper and look for duds. It was late when we went to bed, and I slept as I usually did.

Phu's father's voice broke into my sleep. Mother and Daddy were up and sitting in the former god-room drinking coffee as I hazed to consciousness. Mr. Nguyen was very agitated and repeatedly shouted up the stairs at us through the open slatted window. In broken French he shouted, "Beau-coup veecee! Beaucoup veecee!"

Daddy jumped up. "VC?"

"Oui, oui, beaucoup veecee," Mr. Nguyen shouted back, sweeping his hand in wide arc over his head indicating a universal presence.

Daddy grabbed the little transistor radio off the shelf and tuned to Armed Forces Radio. He was bent over the radio, rolling the dial back and forth with his thumb, each hand dwarfing its size and sound, when I stumbled out of the bedroom trying to pull on my pants.

"What's going on?" I chirped.

I sensed this was it—excitement, real war. Not war off in the distance, haunting my night time, but right here in the daylight. We sat there listening to the radio, trying to find out what it was that was going on. Mother and Daddy discussed the number of choppers they had heard through the night, ". . . many more than usual . . . all night long . . . probably some sort of special exercise over the river." They were wrong.

We weren't especially nervous, though; whatever it was would be no problem for us and the ARVN to clean up. After a rather dull morning of sporadic news I finally gave up trying to get the radio away from Daddy and went out to sit on the stairs. It was not long before Phu showed up all excited, having just come back from the front road. He said that there was a roadblock out there manned by American GIs. At this news we all decided to take a walk and see what was going on. Daddy picked up his movie camera, put on his wrist strap so the camera would not get stolen, and then he, Mother, Phu, and I walked down the lane to the big road. Daddy was hoping to get some information from the GIs and shoot some pictures for our prayer letter. Phu and I wanted to see some action. I don't know what Mother wanted.

We were standing in the middle of the road talking to the roadblock guys when a little posse of GIs came out from a side road and started searching down the street.

"Where ya going?" I asked.

"We had a report that there were some shots around here," the leader drawled as he sauntered off with an M–16 slung nonchalantly over his shoulder. Obviously there was little to worry about, so I started following him down the street. Daddy filmed me for a moment, then called, "Hey! Pal. Don't go so far." Phu and I walked back and were standing around just being part of the scene when we heard a gunshot somewhere nearby. We ducked behind a tin fence and squatted down. It was just a flash, but it put everybody on guard. Before we could all settle on what it meant or where it came from, a Vespa driven by a Catholic priest came swerving unsteadily down the road and right toward the roadblock. The priest could not have chosen a worse moment. The GIs, still nervous from the recent gunshot, spread their legs and waved him to a stop. On the back of the Vespa was a small Vietnamese man with a bandage over one eye. His eye was bleeding through the bandage. The priest spoke in urgent tones and motioned down the road. The big GI, the size of three Vespas himself, had his orders, nobody in or out of Saigon and this roadblock was the cutoff point.

"This here is the secured perimeter of Saigon," he explained. "You hear me, Padre?"

The young priest remained insistent as Phu and I edged into the circle of action. Finally, between Phu's English and my help on vocabulary, we began to interpret. The priest said to Phu who said to me who said to the GI, "This man has been shot in the eye and needs to go to the doctor across the bridge . . . they have some papers here . . . let's see. . . ."

"Look, I don't care if its Colonel Ky himself, he ain't goin' nowhere," the Three-Vespa GI snorted.

The wounded man sat motionless, his shoulders hunched forward, one hand on the priest's shoulder to steady himself, the other hand cupped over his bleeding eye. Obviously, he was hurt bad. Phu and I volunteered to accompany the Vespa past the checkpoint to the GI's sergeant who was standing about a hundred yards down the road. With this much military around, Daddy agreed I could go. We would be in sight and the situation seemed well under control. Besides, this guy needed immediate help. Exasperated, the GI waved us through, and the priest pushed off, wobbling to keep his balance as he drove slowly beside me and Phu.

Excited to be a part of something, we approached the wary-eyed sergeant, and Phu and I started through the whole thing again. We were standing there, about the third time through the whole story, when gunfire exploded all around us. The sergeant and a couple of GIs hit the ground and rolled toward the side of the road. Phu and I vaulted straight into the first space we saw, an open door in a little house right beside the road. We slammed the door behind us and crouched down in the corner beside a little brown cabinet. When my eyes adjusted to the dim light, I saw a Vietnamese family, two parents and a half dozen children, all squatting on their haunches under the kitchen table, which was big enough to really shelter only about half of them. Their dog, an undistinguished short-haired mongrel, stood quivering about two feet from me, its teeth bared, saliva dripping off the lower jaw, its growl even and sustained. For a split second I was more afraid of the dog than the firefight. I was startled back to myself when M–16s split the air in a burst of fire, momentarily covering the screaming, yelling, and commanding of the GIs and the panicked screams of the family's baby. Huddled in that corner, my body pressed against the tile floor with Phu next to me and slightly above, I waited. It might have been ten minutes, it might have been thirty. There was no place to go, nothing to do. We were trapped.

As M–16s lit up another moment of silence with crisp deadly noises I realized that something was happening that was much bigger than me. The pebbled concrete wall made a relief map out of my cheek and forehead, and my knees ached from my frozen posture. If this had been freeze tag I would have wobbled and fallen a long time ago but now I remained perfectly still. Waiting. Periods of silence mixed with gunfire close by eventually gave way to more distant sounds as the firefight moved on down the street. Finally, it was quiet except for the sound of Phu's breath in my ear and the mongrel's quiet growl.

I whispered to Phu, "What are we gonna do?"

"Let's wait," he said.

A few more minutes of silence passed. The air was now filled with that kind of eerie noiselessness that one hears after a disaster, when life has stopped and people stare, one hand covering the mouth in disbelief. The family under the table was still under the table, though the father used this break to pull the dog away from me. In return, I gave him one of the most genuine smiles of my life.

Gradually Phu and I, responding in the same moment, rose awkwardly. We stood up, almost ten feet high if you stacked us end on end, but rather less if you did not. The little house had a Dutch door, just like the nursery door at Cedar Avenue Baptist Church, where the attendants could hand over little babies without the toddlers escaping. Ever so quietly Phu and I stood behind the door and unlatched the top half. I swung it slowly inward and carefully peeked out into the street. There was nothing in sight. There was no Vespa or priest or his shot-in-the-eye passenger and no GIs lying in the gutter. My peripheral vision picked up a blur before I heard the noise of a jeep with three GIs in it come roaring by. The guy in the back turned his head just as they passed, and he looked into the doorway of a small hut and stared a thirteen-year-old American boy right in the eye. We locked for a moment, then he was gone. It must have taken a moment for it to sink in to him that he should not have seen a little white face in there. When he did, he started screaming, "Stop! Stop! Stop!"

The tires squealed a long patch of Goodyear, and the driver ground the jeep into reverse, making it sound as if he was wrenching off two or three gears as he did. The jeep high-whined it backwards and stopped quick in front of the door. Instinctively I ran out to it.

"What the hell are you doing here, kid?" the guy in the back shouted.

"I'm an American, and we live just down the road. Can you give me a ride home?" I shouted back. I don't remember any gunfire just then, but shouting seemed the thing to do, especially since I was polite, and I knew to shout when shouted at.

"Hop in! Let's go!" he shouted.

"Wait," I yelled, "Can he come too?"

"Who's he?" he asked, narrowing his eyes to look at Phu.

"He's my friend. He's okay; he lives at the same place."

He nodded his head and Phu and I leapt over the back lip of the jeep. Before our butts hit the bottom of the jeep, our heads were whipped back as the driver gunned it. As he floored it, the driver turned his head to me and said, "Where to?"

I poked my head between the two seats splitting the front of the jeep and pointed the driver toward the long driveway heading into our house. It was rapidly approaching (just behind the tin fence that we had earlier ducked behind), but the jeep cornered right on target. Pulling into our courtyard, the guy in the back jumped out and crouched down, pointing his M–16 up into the palm tree tops, quickly, evenly, one at a time. There was already another jeep parked next to The Crusader with a guard fidgeting nearby. I sprinted up the steps two at a time, passing a GI on the porch, and burst into the living room. Daddy saw me from across the room and yelled, "You all right, Pal?"

"Yeah, I'm fine," I said. There was no time for rejoicing at the homecoming, no time to kill the fatted calf.

"We've got five minutes to get out," Daddy called, "I've got Bibles, passports, toothbrushes, and the flashlight." There was no barrel to pack this time, no school books, no clothes, no decisions to be made. Nothing to do but get out.

Mother, Daddy, and I hurried back down the stairs and we all gathered at the jeep next to The Crusader. The conversation was drowned in a roar of a Huey skimming over the palm trees. As soon as it was gone, we could again hear the instructions of the head GI: "Get in and stay close. We will put one jeep in front and one behind." He said each word with precision and did not repeat it.

I barely had time to say good-bye to Phu before climbing into my familiar spot in The Crusader. Daddy driving, Mother in the middle, and me hanging out the passenger window. Once we were inside, Daddy told me that the jeep that found me had actually been looking for me on that road. When the firefight broke out, the GIs at the other end had escorted Mother and Daddy back to the house and radioed someone to look for me down the road. Turning out of the driveway, I saw the house disappear behind the wall. It was then that it hit me. I was evacuated to safety. Phu was left behind.

Half a mile down the road we sped, Daddy tailgating the jeep the whole way. The dust from the side of the road billowed up from under the jeep's right wheels and gritted between my teeth. We parked in a small Army base near the bridge and promptly became a problem for everybody in sight. I was sent upstairs to the rec room and given a cream soda while Mother and Daddy went to talk to the base commander. The rec room was air-conditioned, a luxury we did not have back at the house. A couple of GIs were shooting pool when I came in, and my escort told them to keep an eye on me until my folks got back.

One leaned over the pool table, preparing for a long shot, and asked, "Hey kid, you got any sisters?"

"Yeah, I got two," I replied. "They're both married."

"Oooh, too bad, kid, I could make 'em happy. Real happy."

The other GI butted in, "Leave him alone." Then turning to me he said, "Don't mind him. Where you from, kid? . . . and what are you doing in this hellhole?"

I told him my folks were missionaries and we had been evacuated from down the road. The word "missionary" clouded over the face of the guy readying to shoot. He raised his head and looked at me, then he threw down his cue on the table with a rattle and left. I took up the nice guy's offer to shoot some pool, something I had never done before.

After the third time I had accidentally shot the white ball into the pocket, Mother and Daddy came in and said we were joining a convoy into Saigon because they had found another base where we could stay. The consensus was that there were going to be too many fireworks that night to stay in our own neighborhood, even at this base. It was going to be too hot a show to have civilians around. The convoy was going to leave whenever the daily supply truck came, and we, along with an armed escort, would accompany it on its return to Saigon. The rest of the afternoon I sat in the second-story window looking across the river. Off toward Tu Duc I could see a column of smoke rising and flattened off at the top.

Time seemed to have been suspended, and we were stuck somewhere between last night's celebration and today's attack. Counterpoised within such a small amount of time, these events made no sense. I had felt this sense of time stopping only once before, when I was with Daddy as he visited a funeral parlor.

San Bruno

Mother had gone back to work to help put Carolyn through Moody Bible Institute, and Daddy was taking care of me that day. Since it was too hot to wait in the car he thought it would be better for me to come inside.

"Remember, Pal," he counseled as he shut the VW door, "Mr. Thompson is in heaven with Jesus; just the body that he lived in while he was here on earth is inside. There is nothing to be afraid of, although Mrs. Thompson might cry when she sees me because she misses him."

It did not occur to me to ask why somebody might cry when they saw Daddy. I did it sometimes myself. Once we were inside, Daddy talked quietly with some people on the other side of the room. I sat motionless and stiff in my chair, just like the old man in the coffin, and felt the stuffy air choking me. Immediately I wanted to go, but we couldn't because Daddy was not done spending time with the family. That is when I realized with a little panic that something had happened to time. It had stopped, and I was caught in eternity right with dead Mr. Thompson in the funeral parlor.

Saigon

After a long, still wait in the rec room, it was near dinner time when we were beckoned down to the parking lot to join the convoy—two jeeps in the front, then The Crusader, then the supply truck, then two more jeeps. Men stood around clipping clips into their guns, spitting onto the pavement, and waiting. The head of the convoy came up and decided to put me in the jeep right in front of The Crusader. I was to sit behind the GI riding shotgun. Shotgun was already sitting in the jeep, one foot on the dash, one finger on the trigger.

"Son," said the commander, "this is your jeep. Hop in the back beside that box."

"Yes, sir," I quipped as I hopped in, "I'll hide behind the box."

"I'm sorry son, but that there is a box of gauze," he said, pointing with a half-crooked finger. "It's not going to stop any gook bullet." Dismayed at his perceived ignorance of me (after all "Gauze" was stamped right on the side), I joked, "I know *that*, I'm just hoping they don't see me down here."

Spinning away on the toe of one boot, he snapped, "Okay men, our biggest enemy is the unknown. Sniper fire. Heads up. Let's roll."

The MPs pushed the iron gate back and the little convoy of supplies and missionaries crunched through gravel and onto the street and headed toward downtown. As soon as we got up to speed, we drove like madmen. We had not gone quite halfway when we encountered an ARVN roadblock preventing any entrance into the city. Being Americans we had been automatically waved past the first roadblock near our house. This ARVN sergeant was as determined as Three-Vespa GI had been earlier to prevent passage. The whole convoy came to a halt, and we instantly became sitting ducks. The sergeant in the first jeep stood up and, holding the windshield with one hand, he waved to the Vietnamese sergeant to roll back the barbed wire and let us through. The Vietnamese sergeant looked at the American sergeant with a look of noncompliance. I straightened up from my slouched cover behind the box to get a good look at this exchange.

Not wanting to be standing up in plain view of snipers, the American sergeant jumped out of the jeep and jogged straight ahead, firing bursts of profanity as if his mouth were a loaded M-16. "What the hell is going on here? Move that wire . . . NOW!" But the ARVN sergeant held his position. The American sergeant kept right on running dead ahead, and then, to the whole convoy's amazement, hurdled the barricade, getting his gun, his boots, and his beer belly over in one clean jump. This guy was serious. Once on the other side, he reached down, grabbed the rolls of wire with his bare hands, and pulled them off to the side of the road. The ARVN sergeant watched without expression. Once there was enough room to get through, the American sergeant waved to his driver and swung back into his jeep as it rolled by. The ARVN sergeant stepped aside, having done his job all the way up to the point of not shooting an American soldier.

The sun was setting when we wound through some side streets and came to another small compound. Here we would spend the first few nights of the Tet offensive.

11
The Scream

Saigon

We pulled up in front of one of the six million iron gates in Saigon and Roadblock-Hoppin' Sergeant talked to the MP. The gates seem to open automatically as he pointed Daddy to drive through. I hopped out of the jeep, waved good-bye to Driver and Shotgun, and followed The Crusader in. The convoy pulled off and the gates creaked shut behind me.

We had arrived late but were given dinner in the officers' mess. We were shown a table in the corner beyond a long table where all the officers were eating quietly. Their heads lowered and their bodies bent forward, they were listening to a guy at the end of the table. In a few minutes the guy who had been talking got up and came over to our table. He put his hand on my shoulder and said, "Good evening folks. I am Major Williams, base commander. We're glad you can be with us. I hope you will be safe here."

Looking up at him, I saw that gray hair flanked each ear and his eyebrows curled up backwards to his forehead. I was not sure, but I did not think his face seemed very convinced of our safety, though his hand was reassuringly firm. Daddy started to explain how we got there and to thank him for the assistance.

"After dinner," Major Williams interrupted, obviously already knowing how we happened to get on his base, "I will have Sergeant Boone show you to your quarters and instruct you as to security procedures."

Just as he finished he noticed Daddy's flashlight sitting on our Bibles near the foot of the table. He looked positively amazed and said, "Hey! A flashlight. We could sure use one of those at the office. We don't have one to use in blackouts. Could I borrow that?"

Daddy, who was the commander of our family, was not thrilled at giving up something so crucial. I actually think he would rather have given him one of our Bibles, especially since we had three among us and the Major probably needed one anyway. It was one of the few times that I saw Daddy stumble with words, caught between conflicting duties and left straddling the boundaries of politeness and responsibility. Major Williams was politely insistent, and Daddy finally relented on the promise that we would get it back when we left.

After we ate a bowl of vanilla ice cream, Sergeant Boone showed us the air-conditioned bar where we could get free soda pop and then led us to our room at the back of the base. "This is a small base," he explained, "only forty-two men, and we keep a low profile in this neighborhood, given the nature of our job and all." (He did not explain their job but it was obviously some sort of intelligence or analysis thing.) "Administrative offices in front, mess hall in the middle, and then this courtyard surrounded, as you can see, by the finest accommodations this side of Hawaii. Let's see, you all will be in here."

He stepped up onto the sidewalk and opened a green door in a white wall. When he flipped on the light, I saw three single beds, two in the front half, one in the back blocked off by three wardrobes. My bed was the one in the back, and it stood under a window. The low sunlight streamed through the window and lit up each of the little silver buttons on the mattress. A door beside the bed stood open onto a bathroom to be shared with the three guys in the adjoining room.

Since we had no gear to store, he began immediately with "Okay, now let's go over the security arrangements. We are not sure of the situation right now and are waiting to see how this thing develops. During the day feel free to find your way around the base, get a beer, uh, er, a pop over at the canteen and eat in the mess. You are welcome to relax here in the courtyard. After dark, stay in this room and do not leave for any reason unless you are told to do so. Is that clear? Okay. Have a good evening, folks."

After he left, I went to the back of the room and sat on the edge of my bunk. There was no lack of conversation among us. "I wonder what's going on?" "What do you think they know back home?" "What are we going to do now?" "How long do you think we will be here?" The answers ranged over very narrow explanatory ground, from "don't know" all the way to "only the Lord knows." None of them alleviated the swelling on my insides that made me feel like I was holding my breath, even though I wasn't. It started getting dark and I got up and knocked on the bathroom door. Hearing only silence, I went in, and when I pulled on the light chain dangling in the middle of the room, I was immediately blinded by the whiteness of tile. I took a long time to use the toilet, fiddling with the handle and my pants and shirt. Delaying as long as possible, I listened at the door to the other room. There was no sound.

We decided to go to bed, and Daddy turned off the light. For the last five months I had slept with Mother and Daddy. Technically I had a bedroom at our apartment at the Nguyens and when Phu came over, or we had company, I always said, "This is my bedroom." But I had never slept in it. Arriving the first night to bursts of gunfire down by the railroad bridge, Daddy decided he did not want us sleeping in different rooms. We would stick together. Besides, the bed in their room was much bigger than their double bed back home anyway. I had often wanted to sleep in *that* bed with them in earlier years and on scarier nights.

San Bruno

As a child I had a dream: I am a missionary jungle pilot and have crashed in the bush where no white man has ever gone before. Indians with spears emerge out of the bushes, painted and chanting; they poke me with long feather-tipped spears. As I am led into a clearing I see a large black cauldron boiling over a huge fire. I am dinner. I awake just as they pick up my writhing and screaming body and throw me up into the air heading right for the boil. On nights like those Mother and Daddy would never refuse me the security of the parental bed. But to discourage this as I got older, they made me sleep between them. After a few minutes of peaceful bliss, Daddy would gently roll toward the middle, creating, from my view, a wall several feet high. Scrunched between their backs, I knew my oxygen would soon run low, and I felt smothered and miserable. It usually did not take but a few minutes before I decided that my bed was not so bad after all, and I would climb out the bottom of their bed and head back to fresh air even if it was populated by head-hunters.

Saigon

In our apartment in Gia Dinh, Daddy and I slept on the edges, and Mother slept in the middle. I don't ever remember discussing it; it was just part of life since coming here, though Daddy suggested we not talk about it with the other missionaries. Now, lying in my bunk in the dark, I was feeling very far away from them, much farther than the measurable distance of fifteen or so feet. Unable to sleep, I got up and walked over and asked Mother if I could sleep with her.

I was not asleep long before machine gun fire broke out on the base, and I jumped right through my skin. I crouched down at the foot of the bed near the door and listened to the confusion and fear swelling outside.

"This is it, boys!" screamed Major Williams as the swearing and gunfire crescendoed in the courtyard. I opened the door and peeked out. "What are you doing opening that door?" hissed Sergeant Boone as he crawled on his belly across the lawn in front of our room. "Shut that door!" I shut the door and I listened. Daddy was leaning forward, rocking slightly on the bed, and Mother was, as usual, shrugging it all off with an air of indifference. I heard our protectors whispering as they lay on the sidewalk in front of our door.

"Boone, where are the weapons?"

"I don't know, sir. They are not in there."

"Are you telling me that there are forty-two American military personnel on this base and there are only three rifles? Sergeant Boone, is that what you are telling me?"

"Yes sir. Of course, the guards have theirs."

"This is hell, Boone."

"Yes sir."

Oh great, I thought. "Did you hear that Daddy?" I asked.

"Yeah," he quipped. "No wonder they needed the flashlight so bad."

"What time is it?" I whispered.

Daddy held his wrist up to catch a glimmer of light flirting with his watch. "It's three-thirty."

Too wired to sleep and too tired to talk, we fell into silence as did the men in the courtyard. We would have to wait till morning to find out what happened. Squatting by the door, I sat back on my haunches Vietnamese style with my knees in my hands and my head resting on my hands. I stared at the concrete between my tennis shoes. Sometime in the last half hour without being aware of it I had put on my shoes, though I did not have to get dressed because we had been sleeping in our clothes. The floor had little pockets of cement chipped out from things dropped and boots kicked. After my eyes fully adjusted to the dim light, I focused on one little crater about the size of a silver dollar where an ant was at the bottom exploring each crevice. The ant's antennae swirled and poked, its body turned and jerked, stopped, and started. I could see where this ant had come from, I could see where it was going. I could see right where it was and why it could not get out of this little hole. Was this the way God was looking at us right now?

The thought of God translated into spontaneous prayer. We had prayed before bed, and Daddy had read from the Bible, but that was his doing, and it was somehow too formal in the middle of all this, sort of like saying a Thanksgiving dinner blessing when you were just having half a cheese and ketchup sandwich. Now my prayer came from the same place in my chest that kept swelling up:

"Take care of Conrad, Lord. Please let me see him again, Lord. Keep us safe, Lord. Watch over Phu and Huong and their family, Lord. . . . Lord . . . Lord. . . ."

I ran out of words to continue, and my chest burned from holding in the words I had already thought. I opened my eyes and saw that the ant was gone. It was time to lie back down. The next thing I knew, it was morning, and Daddy was shaking me out of bed for breakfast.

The next few days at this compound were much the same. We watched a little TV in the room next to ours. Things were bad everywhere, but the casualties were running twenty to one in our favor. We were killing them. We heard a report that it was bad at Ban Me Thuot. We had recently met a missionary from there at the C&MA guest house, a single girl named Betty Olsen. Daddy said we would have to pray for her and the rest of the missionaries there. (We did not know then that many were already dead, or that Betty Olsen had disappeared into the jungle, kidnapped by the VC to die a torturous and prolonged death of starvation and dysentery.) By contrast, we were on a holiday. Mother always said that somebody had it worse. And now Daddy said that there was no need to be afraid. The Lord was with us. He had promised, especially to us missionaries, "Lo, I will be with you always, even unto the end of the world." I *will*, he said, and this *was* the end of the world. The straightforwardness of the verse was so simple, only a liberal could not see it for what it was—a literal promise from the mouth of God.

The second night brought another firefight early in the morning. This time the gunfire came from the front of the compound. I rushed to put on my shoes, fumbling with the laces in the dark, and then froze, waiting for instructions. Would they leave us sitting through a false alarm like last night or would they tell us something? I nervously looked under the bed and found an Army helmet on a footlocker.

"Daddy, can I wear this, do you think?" I asked, looking for permission to use another person's property.

Daddy smiled. "Sure, Pal, why don't you try it?"

I put it on and it came down over my nose and weighed a ton. Daddy burst out laughing at the sight of my little body dwarfed by this thing. It was so heavy it made my head sway as I fiddled with the strap. Sitting in the dark, my body jumped every time the guns blazed and the unfastened strap slapped me sharply across the face.

I jumped again when someone knocked on the door. Daddy took one giant stride and swung the door back. He looked into the darkness for a split second before he saw Boone crouched down in the doorway.

"Let's go," Boone said. "We're putting everybody together in the offices. VC are at the front gate. Get down and be quiet. Follow me."

Boone went first, followed by me, then Mother, and then Daddy. We waddled like mute ducks through the courtyard and up to the mess. We had to go through the mess to get to the offices, which was unfortunate because the mess door squeaked. Boone slowly reached up and balanced himself on the screen door. He opened the other so slowly that it did not squeak. It was a miracle; the Lord *was* with us. Machine guns spat on the other side of the building by the gate and then fell silent, the guards not knowing who was on the base and who was trying to get in. Crawling below the windows in the mess, we wrapped our way around table legs and through stacks of chairs as we headed for the side door, which led to the shortest route across open space, a parking lot, to administration, where the whole base had gathered with the entire cache of three rifles. The view in the bottom of the mess hall reminded me of the view from under the dining room table at Pinecrest, where I would hide during rubber-band fights with Conrad. I found it a useful place because there were so many legs that it was hard for him to shoot me without the rubber band being deflected.

"Okay," whispered Boone, "we are going to run across here, but stay down." We got up from our waddle, and when he motioned us through the door we bent over from the waist and ran past two parked jeeps and up a short flight of stairs. Just as we hit the top stair the door opened and we ran right in and hit the floor. Boone followed us in and the soldier behind the door shut and bolted it. The action in the parking lot caused the front gate to erupt in continuous fire. From inside our room a scout at the window yelled, "Here they come!" I raised up to look over the table when a friendly hand pushed my head down to the floor in an unfriendly way. The voice at the other end of the hand tensely yelled at me in a whispered panic, "Keep your head down. Ya wanna get it shot off?" Major Williams' voice emerged from the corner and said, "All right, call 'em in."

Underneath the desk right in front of me, a radio guy, released to do what he had been waiting for, began yelling hysterically into a big walkie-talkie. "This is Sammy 4! Sammy 4! Do you read me? We need gunships! Gunships!" The radio cracked back. I could not understand the codes, but the messages coming back were not encouraging Radio-Man.

Spitting curses like brown tobacco juice, Radio-Man's words splattered against my ear and ran down my neck. "We're going down! We need them ... !" He was screaming now, no silence to be observed over the gunfire. The radio squawked more discouraging words, no gunships to be had— it would be half an hour. Radio-Man was hoarse from screaming, "Gunships! Gunships!" but it did no good. We were going down.

The gunfire stopped in a quick break of silence that had its own sound. All I could hear was a woman wailing the high thin-pitched wail of death. My stomach turned slightly as we listened. No words were spoken in the sweat-filled room as the woman's grief pierced the air like a bullet, aimed at every person there, hitting me just below the heart. She did not stop. Finally, a message came into us that she was leaning on the gate begging for help. Opening the gate was the last thing Major Williams wanted to do, but the woman's voice had carried her soul among us. The forty-five of us being now forty-six, she could not be left outside. Besides, it had been quiet for a long while.

Softly and tenderly he called, "Open the gate and let her come in." And then he growled, "But shoot like hell if anything else moves."

From my position on the floor I heard the gate squeak open and then smash closed. Major Williams sent Boone to escort the woman to the mess hall and assign a guard to her. In a few minutes Boone returned and talked quietly to Major Williams while we all listened to the woman's muffled rasping howls in the background. Major Williams came over to where we were lying on the floor.

"Excuse me, Reverend Peters," he said. "Could you come with us?"

Daddy got up, and Boone took Mother and me into the next room and assigned each one of us a metal desk to hide under.

"You think these things will stop a bullet?" I asked Boone plunking the gray metal with my knuckle.

"Between Pittsburgh steel and all that Army paperwork in the drawers, you should be okay under there, kid," he said.

"Oh, I'm sure we will, thank you," Mother replied cheerfully.

Doubled up under the desk, protected by forty-two American military men with three rifles, we waited in the darkness. The howling, hasping screams continued to rise and fall. There was no rhythm to the symphony of grief, just the shattered cacophony of the mother. Tense, alone, we waited for Daddy to come back. Once before in my life I had been in a spot like this.

San Bruno

Mother and Daddy were both at church, and the older kids were gone because now I was old enough to stay alone. It was windy outside, and I could hear the eucalyptus trees whistling and cracking at the top of the hill. I suppose most kids who stayed home alone watched TV, but television was an on-again-off-again thing in our house. First, Daddy would relent to my begging and Mother's subtle hints on my behalf and pick up a used set out of the want ads. Then he would see me get addicted and not be able to turn it off without whining, or he would see something on there that was bad and, pop! that would be the end of it. The TV was gone.

This particular night was during a no-TV spell, so I had the radio on and was reading half-heartedly from a pile of Danny Orlis paperbacks with worn covers. Sitting in my usual upside-down position on the couch, feet on the back cushions and my head hanging off backwards toward the floor, I heard a sound in the basement. My attention ran down the stairs and stopped at the bottom landing to listen. There it was again. Unmistakable. Somebody was rattling the lock on the basement door. I rolled off the couch and went over to the window, gradually cranking it open without a sound. Leaning my face out into the wind I bent as far over as I could to see who might be down there. In the darkness I could see no one, but I knew he was there.

Pulling back in, I ran from lamp to lamp and light switch to light switch, turning each one on. Then I cranked up the hi-fi so that it boomed over all the house. The burglar knows somebody is home now, I thought. I sat on the edge of the couch for a moment giving him time to get away before I leaned back out into the storm to look down in the abyss of the backyard. It was still too dark, and with the hi-fi blaring, I could not hear the lock being jiggled anyway. Cautiously I went over and turned down the hi-fi and waited in the brightened living room. My heart jumped when I heard it again. He was still out there trying to get in. I went over to the phone to call Carmen and Roger, who lived in an apartment not far away, but I had a hard time getting my shaking finger in the little hole of the dial. Roger answered calmly and told me that Carmen was on her way over to our house to do their laundry. There was nothing to do but see who would win this race, Carmen or the burglar.

Waiting for that outcome was too much. I braved going to the back of house and found Conrad's single-shot bolt-action .22. I was not allowed to know where the bullets were, even though I suspected that Daddy probably kept them locked in that box in the closet; but I could never get it open anyway, so that would do no good. I carried the empty gun down the hallway and staked out my position. Think. If he got into the basement, he would come up the stairs into the house. The kitchen was directly across the hallway from the basement door. That is the door he would have to open and come through. I circled through the dining room back to the kitchen and lay on the linoleum floor behind the cabinets. Think. He would not know I did not have a loaded gun, so I would have to shout just the right words. *Stop, or I'll fire!* I thought. Yep, that will do. I practiced it over and over again, though not too loudly in case I could not hear him coming up the steps.

This was a perfect position. I could point the rifle right at the door but keep almost my entire body behind the cabinets. The wind kicked up and blew. While I lay there waiting for that door to open, I noticed that the linoleum speckles made a little pattern like a dull kaleidoscope in dim light and under the ridge of the cabinet I saw a peanut that Mother's broom had missed. Finally, after what seemed like several hours of siege, I heard the door of Carmen's Tempest slam shut. I edged over to the wall and up to the window to look out. Carmen was carrying a big basket across the front lawn with a white sheet flapping on the top.

I burst through the door and met her on the porch with a stream of unstoppable words blowing too hard against her to be heard in the already stiff wind.

"What?" she said when we were once inside with the door shut and locked behind us.

"There is somebody on the back porch trying to get in the basement door!" I spurted.

"It's probably just the wind." she said. "Let's go down there and look."

"No!" I shouted back at her. "He's down there."

"Danny, I have to. I have to do the laundry. Come on."

Carmen opened the basement door, stomped down the steps, flipped on the porch light and thrust open the back door. The garbage can lid had blown off and was resting against the back of the door. When she opened the door, the lid spun away like a top and then circled down with a rattle. She looked at me, and I said, "Somebody was out there."

Saigon

After more than an hour under the desks, Boone finally brought Daddy back in to get us.

I was quiet, but Mother asked, "What happened, Johnny?"

Daddy started to respond and then choked. He stopped, and then with a despair that I had never before heard in his voice, he said, "A lady . . . she was out after curfew . . . was holding a baby in her arms . . . the shot hit the child in the head. . . . She carried the dead baby in here and they laid it on the table in the mess hall but it was too late. There was nothing I could do, I can't even speak Vietnamese to comfort her. That's what they wanted me to do, but I couldn't."

The next day, there was not much to do. I wandered around the base and picked up bullets, lead pieces bent into odd-shaped lumps from their ricocheting travels between the buildings.

12
Guided Missile

Saigon

The next morning Daddy went over to Major Williams' office to tell him about the Littletons and the Moens, C&MA families living across Saigon, to see if they needed to be evacuated as well. Daddy's interpretation of these days was beginning to change. Tet had evolved from an inconvenient interruption of our work into an envelope of events sealing us off from any possibility of a return to normalcy. Events were now in control of us, and within them we could only pray to survive. The wailing woman had visibly sobered Daddy, and after last night I think his theology clarified itself to him. While the Lord was still executing his decrees (which were set before the foundations of the earth), it was becoming clear that those decrees now included some derailment of the work and threatened our very existence. We could die in the crossfire just as easily as that child. We were faith missionaries and would have the final victory, but I had read *Through Gates of Splendor,* by Elisabeth Elliot, widow of the martyred missionary Jim Elliot, and knew that victory for some came by spear. Like most Americans, I believed that God's favor toward us somehow protected us from this kind of danger. After all, on little Sunday school papers I had pasted hundreds of cottonball tails onto pictures of bunnies with "God Is Love" printed across the bottom. Vietnamese Christians were caught in a war in their own land, but we were called by God to come here; that ought to mean *something*.

Passing the afternoon stretched out on the lawn, I was talking with a GI as he polished his captured AK47. It was a chrome-plated North Vietnamese officer's weapon. As we talked, he dipped his rag-tipped finger in a little jar of creamy paste and lovingly rubbed it up and down the barrel of his gun. After it dried, he buffed it till the sun on the barrel glinted, danced, and blinded me as though it were shining on a mirror.

"Baby," he said as he held the barrel like a woman in his arms, "you shine like a '57 Bel Air in the Fourth of Joooly parade."

Daddy's voice interrupted from across the courtyard. "Hey, Pal," he called. "Whatchya up to?"

"Come look at this AK47; it's chrome just like my bike," I called back.

Daddy walked over, and the GI handed him the gun. He turned it over in his hands and inspected it closely. Daddy's love of detail, engineering, and precision appeared briefly in his eyes, but he did not seem as excited as he usually was about unusual guns. Handing the AK47 back to the GI, he started to say something but was silenced as the whole compound began echoing with the sound of an as-yet-unseen helicopter. We looked up, shading our eyes from the sun, standing transfixed by the beat of the blades reverberating up from the ground and resonating in our chests. In an instant it appeared right over us with a gunner perched on a rung on its side. Just as it cleared the base fence the gunner let go with machine gun fire into the block of huts on the far side of us. The roar of the blades and the crack of the machine gun froze and melted me. The helicopter disappeared in a flash, the only sound remaining was of empty shells raining on the tin roof of the mess hall. Rolling off onto the sidewalk they skittered and scattered at my feet. I bent over to pick one up and felt its warmth as though it had a feverish life within.

Daddy's hand on my shoulder herded me back across the courtyard toward our room, where Mother and a newly arrived American man and his Vietnamese wife were watching the sky. Before the sound of the Huey completely faded, it once again began to grow stronger. The copter seemed to be circling and heading for us again. The beat grew stronger and stronger with its coming until it burst right over the wall, spraying bullets and rockets across the sky, cutting it open as if on a dotted line dividing us from the heavens. Each rocket erupted in a stream of white smoke and streaked toward a target just outside the base walls.

The American man began to yell, "That's right, kill the yella' dogs! Let 'em have it. Give it to 'em! Kill 'em."

The intensity of the fight above us and the torrent of jubilant yells from the American man released my own pent-up silences. "Kill the dirty rotten no good VC!" I prayed to the Huey, "Yea! Go get 'em! Kill 'em."

"Pal!" Daddy barked at me so sharply above the firefight that I had no problem hearing him and instantly understanding. Embarrassed at the thought of transacting family business in public, yet not wanting to shame the still-yelling American man, he immediately retreated to a softer tone and whispered, "We don't want anybody to die, Pal."

My insides fell backward into confused silence. I stood there looking skyward, trying to hide the fact that my insides were dancing dances. Dancing the dance of fear to the beat of the Huey blades and dancing the dance of joy to the counterpoint of the rockets' red glare. The Huey made three or four passes and then, as a huge column of black smoke arose from the gas station around the corner, it disappeared. The smoke billowed higher and blacker until it blotted out the sun, and we were left standing in shadow. As the air thinned, Daddy sighed with relief and told me I could go over to the mess hall for a soda.

The mess hall resided in air-conditioned darkness. I sat up on a stool at the bar, and a GI approached with a friendly tone. "I bet you'd like a Coke, kid," he said. "I got a real cold one in here."

I nodded silently, and he poured it into a funny-shaped glass with a bulge at the top. Little beads of sweat popped up on the glass out of nowhere and ran down the sides in rivulets. I took big mouthfuls of Coke and held them, challenging myself to see how long I could take the burning. I could never take it very long before my eyes watered up and my throat swallowed it down. In the background the radio played "House of the Rising Sun," and I tried to picture Phu and Huong back on the riverbank. Before I could locate the memory, the guy behind the bar interrupted with the obligatory first question all displaced Americans ask of each other, "Where you from, kid?" When I left, I was still a little tense and still a little happy that we had gotten 'em.

Under blackout orders we had lengthy devotions by flashlight that night. The narrow beam of light burrowed through the darkness, reflecting shadows off God's Word and onto the Army's wall. We began by reading Romans 8. Near the end of the chapter it was my turn to read. Daddy held the flashlight with a steady hand while I read,

> Likewise the Spirit also helpeth our infirmities: for we know not what we should pray for as we ought: but the Spirit itself maketh intercession for us with groanings which cannot be uttered. And he that searcheth the hearts knoweth what is the mind of the Spirit, because he maketh intercession for the saints according to the will of God. And we know that all things work together for good to them that love God, to them who are the called according to his purpose. For whom he did foreknow, he also did predestinate to be conformed to the image of his Son, that he might be the firstborn among many brethren. Moreover, whom he did predestinate, them he also called, and whom he called, them he also

justified; and whom he justified, them he also glorified. What shall we then say to these things? If God be for us who can be against us? He that spared not his own Son, but delivered him up for us all, how shall he not with him also freely give us all things? Who shall lay any thing to the charge of God's elect? It is God that justifieth. Who is he that condemneth? It is Christ that died, yea rather, that is risen again, who is even at the right hand of God, who also maketh intercession for us. Who shall separate us from the love of Christ? shall tribulation, or distress, or persecution, or famine, or nakedness, or peril, or sword? As it is written, For thy sake we are killed all the day long; we are accounted as sheep for the slaughter. Nay in all these things we are more than conquerors through him that loved us. For I am persuaded that neither death, nor life, nor angels, nor principalities, nor powers, nor things present, nor things to come, nor height, nor depth, nor any other creature, shall be able to separate us from the love of God, which is in Christ Jesus our Lord.

We closed, singing quietly so as to not disturb our new neighbors in the next room, "Turn your eyes upon Jesus / Look full in his wonderful face / and the things of earth will grow strangely dim / in the light of his glory and grace." I fell asleep, the Huey no longer beating in my chest.

I could never tell if I awoke before it hit, or if the impact of the explosion was so sudden that I just imagined being conscious at the time. As I looked straight up, my first vision was of the roof detached and suspended in mid-air nearly a foot off the top of the surrounding walls. It hung, suspended in time for a distinct moment, a moment without time or measure, an envelope into which a lifetime could be compressed, and then thundered back down in a terrifying sound, closing that glimpse of eternity. Chunky clouds of plaster smoked from its cracks and floated down on us like crepe streamers at a birthday party. The sounds of glass breaking and wood splitting overwhelmed and deafened me. We jumped to our feet, pandemonium wrapping its arms around us, someone's screams clutching at my throat. In the darkness somebody was shrieking, "I'm hit! Oh God! God! I'm hit! I'm hit! Somebody help me! Please, help me!"

Daddy leaned over and peered out the window through a slit in the curtains. We knew by now to keep all the lights out inside so we could see out and "they" could not see in. In the darkness I paced rapidly back and forth, spinning and walking, spinning and walking. Running my fingers through my hair as though there might be a strategy in there, I looked for a plan of action. I had to do something. I had to go call for help. I had to get a gun. I had to fight back. We had to protect ourselves and Mother! We had to fight! Fight! Far off I could hear Todd yelling to me, "Fight him, Danny. Fight him."

San Bruno

Mellow Yellow was the weirdest kid at Engvall Junior High. His strangely colored skin was enough to keep him away from us and his Dumbo ears sealed any chance of his having friends anywhere among us, the Engvall Eagles. There were many rumors about his yellow skin: he is sick with a contagious disease; he is Mongolian; he is half Chinese communist and half something worse; his parents are drug-addicted hippies; he is just plain weird. At lunch he always ate alone, and he always walked the perimeter of the playground, keeping away from the basketball courts where we ran and passed and shot and shouted. Sometimes I would look up and see him staring at us. If he saw me, he would dart away. *Man*, I thought to myself, *I'm glad I'm not him.*

On this particular Friday as Todd was encouraging me to fight this guy, I was glad to just be back "in." Todd and the Pinecrest gang would go through these cycles in which somebody on the block was always "out." Except for Todd. He was never out because he was pretty much the one who decided who was in and who was out. Several months earlier I started getting labeled stupid. It started in an argument with Jerry over whether or not cavemen existed. I vehemently denied it on the biblical basis of the creation of Adam and Eve, which obviously precluded apemen in caves somewhere. (*Evidently*, I thought to myself, not too surprised, *you can be Catholic and not believe the Bible*.) Jerry finally appealed to the highest local authority.

"Todd," he asked incredulously, "did you hear this? Peters doesn't believe in cavemen. Is that stupid or what?"

This question caught Todd off guard because it made him the judge between Baptist and Catholic, when he knew both were obviously inferior to Greek Orthodox. Luckily, he stayed out of it, but I got the impression that he thought Baptists were pretty stupid.

Then in algebra Todd could do all his homework while in class and I could not even understand any of the little squiggly marks on the board. He was clearly disgusted with my density. Finally, a couple months later, I swung a baseball bat and hit his little brother on the arm. The whole gang walked home on the opposite side of the street from me, Todd talking loudly so that I could hear, "Boy, is he in for it! I am going to pound his face tomorrow."

That was it. It was all over. I was ejected from the Pinecrest gang for being stupid. It was my introduction to fear. Real fear, not the kind you get from leaving the closet doors open at night allowing the beast to roam, but the terror that was waiting for me in the bathroom or at the drinking fountain. I found notes in my desk saying "Today is the day you are going to get it. Watch out!" When Todd passed out the papers in algebra, he always skipped me so that I would have to raise my hand and ask for one, adding to Mr. James' despair over my work and to my growing image of stupidity. I dreaded coming out of homeroom because our paths had to cross and the whole gang would stop and taunt me. I looked straight ahead and walked stiff-legged to the next class. Eventually I became an expert at finding creative ways to walk home, even if it took an extra half hour. Once safely home I spent the rest of the day in the basement reading Danny Orlis books over and over again. Danny Orlis was a kid like me, a Christian adventurer/detective who was going to grow up and go to the jungles as a missionary.

One really scary day I called Carmen at work, and she left early to pick me up. I waited for her inside the school office while the gang sat on the lawn outside waiting for me to come out. They finally left before she got there, but on the way home we stopped at Littleman's and they were waiting inside. Carmen took off after them, "What's the matter with you boys? I am going to tell your parents." I was mortified, this was going to get me in deeper than ever, and I would never get out.

"Ooooh," they called from the tuna aisle, "Danny's fatso sister is protecting him now. What a sissy!"

Having used up Carmen's freedom to get off work early, I begged my homeroom teacher for a ride home by pleading my case over and over again.

"Why don't you just fight him?" my teacher finally said. "Get it over with. Pound him like a crazy man and he'll run."

"I can't," I whined. "There are four of them and only one of me."

He drove me home shaking his head. I thanked him for the ride, but I still thought he was bonkers for wanting me to fight back.

Conrad finally decided that I needed to learn how to fight. His roommate at college knew karate, and Conrad was going to teach me. "Okay," he said, kneeling in front of me, "I'm going to hold my hands up like this and you punch me in the palms. Make it real quick, with a snap to it."

I looked at him. He was the last person I wanted to hurt.

"Go on," he said, "do it."

"I can't. I don't want to," I whimpered.

Carmen sat on the couch cheering me on. "You can do it, Danny, just hit him like you did Mikey when we first moved here. Remember that? You gave him a bloody nose."

"He was only four," I pleaded.

"Yeah, well, so were you then. Do it again," she encouraged.

I straightened up my outsides and bid my insides to do the same. With a fierce look I gave Conrad's palm a full-fisted punch.

"Yeeoow," I cried, falling to the floor and rolling onto my side. I held my hand with the sprained finger while Conrad rolled his eyes and moaned, "Oh, brother. You've got to keep all your fingers tucked in."

That was the end of my fight training. By this time Todd had made an appointment with me to settle it all in the backyard, but I sent him a note saying I had to go to the dentist. Jerry did not believe it, but Todd said it was an honorable excuse and we would reschedule the fight. Finally, tiring over the cold war, Daddy approached Rob and Todd's older brother, Tim, to help me. They took me to Todd's backyard, and everybody started yelling at once. Todd's mother came out and found out about the whole thing and started yelling at Todd in her Greek accent. "What's the matter with Danny? He's a nice boy. What have you got against him?"

"He's a stupid sissy," Todd yelled back.

I sat silently on a patio chair surrounded by a neighborhood and family argument. Todd's mother finally extracted a promise from Todd that he would leave me alone.

Somehow the nightmare ended and now Jerry was on the "outs." Now Todd said to me, "I don't know how I could have been so stupid to have liked him and not liked you."

"Do you know what stupid thing he did last week?" I responded.

Now here I was, fighting Mellow Yellow, not so much because I had anything to fight him about, but because Todd had told me I should. I was fighting my way back "in." I had never fought Todd, but at least I could show him I could fight. Having thrown two punches in my entire life, one as a four-year-old, which had been very successful, and one at Conrad's hand, which hadn't, I did not risk punching Mellow Yellow. I pushed him down on the ground and sat on his chest thinking to myself, "What am I going to do now?" I finally decided to pull his ears because they seemed big and pullable. Unfortunately, I did not have his arms pinned, and he reached up and, grabbing my ear lobes, pulled right back. His strength and determination surprised me. He was supposed to run away crying by now, but there we sat, deadlocked with gritted teeth and pulled ears, looking right at each other.

"Fight him!" Todd yelled.

"What do you want me to do?" I shot back, hoping the reddened pain of my ears did not show in my voice.

"Do something to him that he can't do to you, dummy," Todd snorted.

Before I could figure out what that could be, somebody yelled, "Teacher!" and I jumped up and walked away.

"Way to go!" Todd congratulated.

I thought to myself, "I fought him, I actually fought." It was not a great bout, but I had done what I had to do. The results of the fight did not vanquish Mellow Yellow. He still sulked around school and now almost seemed a touch defiant. I, on the other hand, was back much closer to the center of the group, though still feeling closer to its bottom edge than Todd even knew existed.

Saigon

When Daddy turned from looking out the window, I stopped pacing back and forth and waited for a report. Just then Sergeant Boone hissed through the door, "Stay in your room and stay down. They're coming through the back gate."

He was gone to the sound of M16s and more yelling. In the dark I looked across at Daddy now sitting on the other bed. He was looking at me, my face covered with plaster powder and little chunks of what had been the wall now entangled in my hair. I sat down on the edge of the bed, round-shouldered and jittery. I tucked my feet up under me, having discovered shards of glass on the floor. Daddy looked at me for a long time, right into my face, almost as though he was longing for something. Later I figured out that it was at that moment he decided to send Mother and me home. I don't know when he decided to stay and carry on the work by himself, but that was when he decided to send us home.

After awhile the night once again quieted down. There were no more explosions, and the wounded guy had been taken away. Eventually Boone came back to our door. "It's over for now," he sighed. "Get some rest, but stay alert. They may try it again."

We did not sleep the rest of the night, and we did not talk much either. When the pink light of dawn came, I got up to go the bathroom. Passing the bunk under the window in the back where I had been too scared to sleep, I saw that the whole window was blown out and big chunks of stuffing stuck out of holes in my mattress. It had been punctured and ripped from mortar shrapnel and debris. The wardrobes separating that back bunk from the other two beds were full of holes, and one door hung ajar. I walked back to Mother's and my bed and noticed that the wall, starting from six inches above where we lay, all the way to the ceiling, was peppered with the pocked marks of shrapnel holes.

13
Footsteps

Những Vết Chân

After breakfast Mother, Daddy, and I joined Boone and Major Williams to inspect the alley behind our room. We discovered that a mortar shell had landed five feet outside our window in an open trash can full of empty pop cans. The trash can still stood, its side ripped open, leaving a twisted and jagged hole. A hundred Coke cans were strewn in bits of red up the alley, like little pieces of guts from a cat run over by too many semis on Bayshore. The Coke cans absorbed most of the explosive energy, otherwise it would have blown us to the kingdom we knew was coming.

After a bit of debate the military men decided it was a stray mortar, an accidental trajectory, and that the base was not really under attack. This information amended the previous night's judgment that since the explosion occurred next to a delivery gate it was the VC blowing it down to come in.

Major Williams concluded with a diagnosis: "No VC attack, folks; it was just a random thing, an accident. It happens in war."

"I don't think so," Daddy said. "That was no random hit; that was a guided missile. One of our guardian angels put it right in the garbage can where it saved our lives."

A couple of the GIs standing there looked up at him but said nothing. Obviously the guy in the next room did not have

141

a guardian angel. This explanation would later be repeated among the missionaries. A miracle for the Peters.

Standing there in the circle of soldiers and missionaries, my arms folded across my chest, I didn't know what to believe. If it was a guided missile, then it was not random. If it was not random, then it meant something. As Daddy often told me, I'm a pretty good thinker. So, if the meaning was to save our lives, why couldn't it have missed by a little more? If it was a guided missile and it *almost* killed us, then maybe there was a message in there somewhere. Was God warning us with: "I can kill you if I want, or I can just scare you half to death to remind you that I can kill you if I want, but I didn't, so be grateful"? If it was guided, then God was here protecting us. Why didn't he protect others? Oh yeah, of course, we were doing his will and they weren't. But then why did we almost die? Are we almost not doing his will? Daddy was right, the meaning here must be that it was a guided missile, so I decided to be grateful.

"Well, Pal," Daddy beamed as we returned from the alley, "praise the Lord."

After having "his" civilians almost get it twice in three days, Major Williams thought it would be a good idea if we were moved to some safer place. He trotted off to the office to find a place for us. Daddy followed him to remind him about the C&MA missionaries across town in order to get them help if they needed it. Mother and I returned to the room and sat on the bed.

The Littletons and their upstairs neighbors had been in Vietnam a long time now, and these wars and rumors of wars were no big deal to them. We were just newcomers getting all excited about nothing. Of course, it had been relatively quiet in their neighborhood during Tet. Boone and two GIs had escorted us over to the Littletons' house in The Crusader, and we sat waiting for them to pack and get going. Unfortunately, Mrs. Littleton was a whiner and decided this would be a good time to whine—about her paintings and her silverware and this and that and how this was not necessary. Jake Littleton had little power over her whining, so we all sat there and listened, Daddy steaming from the insult to the GIs who had volunteered to help us evacuate, only to face a crabby missionary wife. They probably thought she was rather bitchy, but we only thought she was carnal, selfish. Finally, after an interminable afternoon of waiting, the GIs escorted all three families to a new base for security. This base had a couple of hundred people roaming all over inside halls and carrying papers and stuff.

The three families shared two rooms, with a bathroom in the middle. The women were put on one side, and the men on the other. There were people on the single beds and in the chairs and on the floor. Daddy and I were assigned a single bed. After dinner it was announced that there would be a movie shown in the rec hall and everybody was invited. This put our parents in a funny position because we did not watch Hollywood movies. The title of this one, *Follow Me, Boys*, made them all the more suspicious. Daddy decided to find somebody who knew something about the "film" (that's what we called them when we showed them in church, and we never, never called them a show) to see if he would let me see it. The Littleton kids had bad manners, so I figured they would get to see it, but I did not know if I would. It turned out to be a lucky day: a guardian angel had saved my life and then I got to see a movie.

Late in the night, I was alone in my wakefulness amid the three missionary men and the two boys. Daddy's barrel chest rounded upward toward the neon light fixture and rumbled its familiar tones. One hand on his chest and one hand dangling, he slept like he lived—straight. Scrunched between the wall and his body, I was in a splint. I lay there and remarkably thought about very little, not about the movie, not about the guided missile, not about Michele, not about Conrad. I was just lying there listening to the cricket outside the window and the not-so-far-away rumbles of B–52s.

If it hadn't been for the splint, I would have been thrown out of bed by it. It was so sudden, so immediate, so violent, so red and yellow and hot like fire, and so sharp and clean like surgery that it exploded in my head and ran like a long knife straight down into my chest so that my heart stopped mid-beat. Dead stopped. A single scream had come from the row of shacks leaning up against the wall of the base just below our window. It was a woman's scream, and I heard it pure and high and then choke quickly into a garbled stillness. I now knew what a knife through the heart sounded like. I knew what it felt like. Everyone in the room was awakened and lay tense and still and quiet. Mr. Littleton went to the bathroom door and called through to the women to see if they were okay in there.

"Oh yes, we are fine," they said, "but . . . what was that?"

"It was from the little shanties by the fence . . . we don't know," he answered quietly.

The next day the men went back to the house for supplies and when they returned, Mr. Littleton had a different opinion about being evacuated. The dead bodies lining the side of the road on the way to their house had changed his mind.

That day a GI walked up to me and said, "Hey, remember me?" I had never seen his face before. "It's me," he said, "the guy with the chrome-plated AK47." Embarrassed to squelch his joy, I just mumbled something dumb and left him with a hurt look on his face. I did not remember him, only his gun.

Finally, we were sent back to stay at the Littletons' missionary compound. It was safe enough—probably. We were given two old M14s for self-protection and left to fight for our own safety. The Littletons decided to spend the night in the bomb shelter, and we were given the front bedroom. The others would stay in their apartment upstairs. Part of the evening was spent trying to decide how to guard the place, how to distribute the guns, and what we should do if something happened. As the sun set we knew we could not turn on the lights, so we assumed our positions for the night. Daddy sat in a chair near the door in our bedroom. From this vantage point he could cover the front of the house. He sat in a straight-backed chair with the M14 lying across his lap, loaded, the safety off. He kept one hand on the stock and one free to sip cold coffee. Mother and I had to stay away from the window and remain as low as possible; so we lay together in bed, waiting for the night to pass. Ironically, somebody had thought it safe enough for us to return and dangerous enough to provide us with weapons. They had put it something like: "I'm sure you all will be all right, but just in case they come through that part of town, you'd better have weapons." Actually, it was Daddy who went into the office and did not come out until he had the guns.

We lay there and waited, occasionally whispering but not even doing that too often. If the VC moved, it would be at night. If the VC found American missionary families, it would be all over. Daddy was prepared to kill anybody who came after us that night, missionary or no. There were pacifist Mennonite missionaries in Vietnam, but we were fundamentalist Baptists and were used to fighting for what was right. It was right to kill a communist to protect your family, though I do not know if Daddy would have done it just to protect himself. He would rather have been taken captive so he could preach, like the apostle Paul.

About two in the morning, as I was whispering to Mother, we heard a distinct footstep outside one window. Life stopped. We froze. Again. Distinct. Crisp. Deadly. The sound of a knife last night, the sound of crunching leaves and gravel tonight. Each second slowly passed as though unable to overcome the inertia of the fear of what it might bring. Daddy's hand was slow and steady. It moved over the stock and gripped it tight. The other hand lifted the barrel so he could slide his finger around the trigger. The moonlight was dim through the pulled shade but it was enough to see him swing the gun up and level it at the handle of the front door. If it opened, whoever opened it was gonna be dead. The footsteps rounded the corner of the house and paused under the side window, inches from my head. Then gently, carefully, they eased away into the inky night, leaving us to slowly exhale and wait again, for sunshine, or more footsteps.

The next day Daddy moved us back to the C&MA guest house, where we had first landed six months ago.

14
Abandoned

Saigon

The violence took on a regular rhythm. Helicopter blades, clips of AK47s and M16s, earthquakes from the B–52 carpet bombings, sirens, and the fires of Cho Lon burning across the yellow walls were such daily events that in the space of two weeks Tet had evolved from thrill to life-threatening and then to its own distinct kind of life. Upon our return to the C&MA guest house, we found a military fortress. ARVN soldiers huddled behind M50s on the roof and on the balcony that ran across the second-storied front. Our room faced Cho Lon, and we stood in the evenings watching the sky's hellish glow as it burned orange and gold, fueled by gasoline and wood and human flesh. It was a demonic conflagration whose hot breath consumed babies, soldiers, old men's memories, and young girls' dreams. It consumed temples and schools and houses. It consumed civilization. It consumed God himself.

Daddy's dreams for the evangelization of Vietnam, of peace through Christ, were cinder dust in the alley out back. His immediate desire was to return me and Mother to the States, and it was taking up hours of planning each day. Every morning he would be on the telephone or disappearing in The Crusader, trying to find a way out. Boats through the Mekong were too dangerous, and the airport was still shut down. Word was that even once it reopened no commercial planes would

147

come in because of the lack of insurance coverage. In preparation for the day when we would depart Saigon, Daddy decided we had better brave the streets to get back to our apartment at the Nguyens and collect our possessions.

Negotiating the streets of Saigon, we passed a city in silence. Corner gas stations lay in rubble, Perlon billboards hung sideways from their frames, a whole city block of tin huts lay in lumpy flats felled by direct hits and the concussion of nearby explosions. The only thing left standing was the concrete stall of a bathroom, charred sooty black from the fires, except for a little square of still pale concrete down in the back corner where a small body had huddled to await the salvation that never came. Rounding a wide intersection barren of honking taxis and peddling bicycles, Daddy slowed abruptly. In the road ahead, slightly off to the right, lay three unexploded mortar shells. Daddy raised himself off his haunches and strained to look over the hood to scope the entire intersection before choosing a careful path around them. As we passed, I saw the little fins at the back of the shell cast a silent shadow of crenalations in the morning sun.

Nothing is more unsettling than silence where there should be sound. That kind of silence collapses the past and the future into the present moment, and it is too much too bear. It resides inside you on the verge of exploding into sound, a scream of release if nothing else. Gripping the door handle of the Crusader, I crushed silence from knuckles to mouth.

Silvery beads stood out on Daddy's forehead by the time we turned into our driveway. Immediately Phu and Huong came running out to meet us. We greeted in adolescent awkwardness that was soon overcome in an avalanche of words and stories and adventures. They too had experienced close calls. Our house had been directly under fire, and the sky had been lit with fireworks. Several flare parachutes had dropped into the yard, and my Vietnamese friends proudly presented me with one. While Mother and Daddy began sorting through the household goods, Phu and Huong and I went up to the back of the house to see where a new round of explosions was coming from. We stood in the hallway, watching the South Vietnamese Air Force bomb a Catholic church a couple of miles from us. Holing up in churches was a common Viet Cong tactic, just another barbaric way for Communists to destroy Christianity. A line of planes appeared on the horizon, single-engine bombers left over from some earlier American victory and now dispensed to our ally. The drone of the planes built in the palm trees and in the air, vibrating the clear varnished floorboards of the second floor. The lead plane suddenly spun off level flight and fell twisting toward the church like a spiraling bird of prey. Just above the tall spire it pulled up and defecated large bombs from its belly. When they hit, we saw through the silence their long flaming arms of fire and smoke arching away like the legs of a giant spider consuming its prey. The orange and black was captured in a moment of stillness as the exploding arms of fire burst over the church roof. Suddenly the silence itself exploded as the concussion rattled the windows and slapped us sharply across the face. Bomber after bomber after bomber, always with the pause between the explosion and the slap. In that pause there was no war, just Phu and Huong and I looking out the window.

Daddy called to me to pack my suitcase and throw it into the back of the truck. After that, all that was really left to deal with was the kitchen. For some reason I became loud and giddy, and I picked up a quart pot and threw it at Phu. "Here, ya want this?" I laughed nervously. He was so taken aback that he could not speak. Daddy realized how rude I had been and went over to Phu. He took another pan with both hands and, following Vietnamese custom, presented it to Phu, saying, "It would be an honor to give you these kitchen things." I felt remorse and looked down. After promising to write from America, we quietly got into the truck and drove back to the C&MA guest house. I never saw Phu and Huong again.

Practically under house arrest at the C&MA guest house, we were trapped between wars and rumors of wars. Daily we heard new and horrible stories, not knowing what was true and what was not—"*. . . three hundred VC moving across the neighborhood. . . .*" We waited, hoping to hear and hoping not to hear. "*. . . fresh division of VC at the edge of town ready to renew the attack on the airport. . . .*" When the phone rang, we all jumped. "*. . . Betty Olsen is still missing . . .*" We knelt in prayer and waited for the Lord to save. "*. . . Tonight's the night. Be prepared to gather in the kitchen . . .*"

Tet's most wrenching terrors were the stories of what was happening to others—the Ban Me Thuot missionaries, the street fighting, the friends of friends who never came home. The terror of the known and the terror of the unknown. One story I do not know the facts about, the adults withholding them from me. I only know how I took the report, "*. . . one of the Vietnamese pastors has been caught by the VC and hung by his feet in the doorway of the church and skinned alive . . . ,*" and mythologized it into a story too terrifying to imagine, until now.

✳ ✳ ✳

My name is Nguyen Van Cam. I am pastor of Tin Lanh Church in Quan Nam village. I was hung by my feet in the doorway of the chapel and skinned alive for Jesus' sake.

Early in the morning we would meet for prayer, myself and Pastor Vinh. Some mornings as early as 4:00 a.m., while moonbeams dance across the rice paddy, Pastor Vinh and I quietly walk together to the chapel, the only sound rising from the wet grass bending under our feet on the trail. Lately we've had many discussions as to whether we should wait for daylight to come, since the VC had been much more active around our village and had even posted a warning on the church door. "Imperialist swine cooperators will die," it read. But it was clear that the early morning was the time when Jesus prayed, and he would be with us in the chapel as much as in our own beds.

We had much to pray about these days. The war was unceasing. Two of the men in our village were dead, three more had missing limbs and could not farm. The girls were disappearing to Saigon, and the little boys ran and played war. The B–52s ground up the night in their rumbling, and the day was chopped like Nana's pork into minute pieces with the beat of the Huey blades. As much as we tried to live in peace, we prepared for war.

Pastor Vinh and I had just knelt on the concrete floor and bent our heads forward to pray when the wooden door was kicked open. We moved to rise, but before we could stand a man in black slammed a rifle butt against my head and I fell back into a pool of darkness. I awoke a moment later to hear the chatter of four VC standing over us. Pastor Vinh was sitting, blood running from his nose.

"Oh God," I prayed, "help us, help us, help us."

The leader looked over at me and saw that I was awake. He smiled slowly and then his eyes narrowed and he said, "There is no mercy for you. None. Where is your god now, American boy? He must be off on his own filthy business, because he is not here to save you, heh? I am the leader of this band, I am the leader of this village, and I will scour the demons of this god from this place for our father, Ho. You are so stupid you do not even know that the man you called Deacon Luon is one of us. He told us you would be here. And he was right. Now you are going to die."

I started to respond, but a foot to my mouth loosened a tooth and cut my lip.

I spit out the tooth, and the leader laughed in my face, saying, "Hah! A toothless preacher of a toothless god. The oldest woman in this village, with a vagina dried shut from lack of use, has more teeth than your god, American slave!"

One of the other men in black was pacing nervously. The sky was just turning faint hues of coral and papaya from sunrise. Maybe there was promise here, like a rainbow. A missionary friend outside Hue had been very successful talking to VC in the middle of the night in his church. They had even become friends of a sort. Why couldn't that happen now? God had promised to work miracles if we had the faith. My faith has always been strong. It will not fail me now.

The pacing one turned and said, "Let's do it and go. We can get rice and a woman before we go, and it will still be dark. Let's go." With the last words he pulled a knife from his belt and held it up. The tip was broken off and from the lantern's flicker I could see bubbles of rust.

"No," the leader said, "this one is cocky. He will die slowly so that his god has plenty of time to save him, just in case it takes his god a while to find him!"

"Tie them up," he hissed. Then he walked down the aisle toward the door, which was still standing open from his quick kick. I suddenly saw the congregation all sitting before me in last Sunday's service—the men on one side and the women on the other. Little Hou's dog was asleep in the aisle. In the front row was my beautiful bride—married only six months and now showing a roundness to her belly, our first blessing from God. Her face was alight with peace and joy as we sang, "Like a river glorious is God's perfect peace . . ."

Now there was no peace. There was a knot in my stomach. This could not be happening. We were growing as a church, people were being saved, my child was coming, and back in our bed Hoa slept in a cotton shirt of mine, waiting for the dawn, when she would get up and fix me breakfast.

The leader in black interrupted my thoughts as his hand slapped the door post. "Here," he said. "We'll do it here."

I looked up at the double door frame and then to Pastor Vinh. His eyes were frozen, and his breathing was shallow. My body was tingling in tiny little shakes, shakes high and fast, out of the rhythm of my life and the life of this village.

Then slowly, like the sunrise, the scene rose in my mind. They were going to hang us in the doorway and let us swing there until we were found.

"Oh, God! Oh God! Oh God!" I cried. "Please no, God. I do not want to die."

Even as I pleaded with God, they came over and began to tie my feet together and my hands behind my back. They roughly rolled me to my feet and put a blindfold over my eyes. They worked in silence. They worked quickly. Once we were both blindfolded, they took us by the elbows and we hobbled down the aisle. I knew the church by heart so that I knew when we were at the last row. We stood and waited while they made more quiet noises around the doorway.

Suddenly I felt a knife point at the middle of my groin and I flinched. A laugh was all the response I heard, and then I felt the knife cutting down my pants leg and my pants being torn off. They cut away my underwear and I hung openly before them. There were smirks, and one said, "See that little worm! Hah! What can he do with that!" More laughter as the knife struck a gash in my back and my shirt was ripped off. I stood there naked while they did the same thing to Pastor Vinh. He yelped as the knife cut his waistband open.

"You scream one time, and we will put your wives to death too, including the one with the swollen stomach, no?"

"Oh God, Oh God, Oh God." I had no words, just a scream pumping in my heart. Suddenly rage broke out, and I hurled my body toward the presence I felt next to me. I knocked one of them over and heard yelling and screaming. I was kicked in the ribs and then in the groin. I convulsed and spit up blood and bile. The one I had knocked over wanted to kill me right then, but the leader said, "We'll do it slowly, to give his god time to get here. He is probably in America and can't find this poor gook in the Mekong."

They put a gag in my mouth and lifted me to stand. I stood doubled over half in shock. This can't be real. This can't be real. "Where are you, God? Didn't you promise to be with us, to save us, to heal us? Where is the life more abundant? Where is the peace like a river that o'erfloods my soul?" Suddenly enraged at God, I screamed into my gag, "God! God! Where are you?" Nausea swam in my head and I started to throw up into my gag. It caught in my mouth and I had to swallow it back down before I choked on my own vomit. I had just preached on dogs returning to their vomit. Was I a dog in God's sight?

Two of the men began to pick me up very high. I went limp and waited for the noose to go around my neck. But it did not. Instead, they tied my feet to a rope and then yanked me upside down. My head banged on the ground and then on the side of the doorjamb as I swung upside down in the doorway. I could barely breathe, my ribs ached from the kicks, and my throat was choked with rags and vomit. Blindfolded, I hung suspended in the dark, not knowing what was happening and not knowing where God was. I thought of Hoa in our bed, snuggled against the sheets. Was she safe? Had they already raped and killed her? I saw a fleeting image of her loins, opened and exposed with a knife poised against her, cutting just enough to bleed. I began to jerk my body wildly, unable to free myself, unable to save her, unable to . . .

My heart was pounding in my chest and head. "Be calm," I thought. "They are just terrorizing us to make an example to the village. I will be okay. Oh God, please God, save me and I will serve you forever. I will give up all my desires for fame to be Vietnam's leading evangelist. I will be humble and serve you forever. Please God, just let me live."

Exhausted, I hung limp. How long had it been? Fifteen minutes, an hour? I did not know.

The leader finally spoke, "Cam, you will be an example to the whole village. They will see that on the inside you are no different from us. You are not better. You are the same. We all kill for our own reasons. To show the village this, we will show the village your insides, what you look like underneath your skin."

With that I felt a sharp slice on my inner thigh. I cried and tried to struggle, but they held me tight. I was almost passing out from the pain and the blood filling my brain. Fire raced across my thigh as someone slowly peeled my skin back and cut at it in little swipes. A cut, a swipe just under the skin and then he would pull. I was dizzy and nauseated and wretched.

"GOD, GOD, GOD, GOD, GOD!"

No answer. Just another cut as my leg felt the breeze blow across the blood, cooling the fire but making it feel worse all the same.

Blood ran down my torso and over my neck. It ran into my hair and clotted. I began to shake in shock and drifted in and out of consciousness. They cut the nipples off of my chest and skinned my stomach.

I was going to die. No one could save me. Even if God showed up now, he could not save me. God had let me die. This was the last thing I knew. God had abandoned me right there under the sign that read "Good News." He had died for me, what was this I was having to do? Do I pay for my own sin? I begged God to let me die, but I did not die. First I begged him to let me live and he did not. Now I begged him to let me die, to escape this skinless body, but he did not. He let me hang between life and death, with pain screaming at me and torturing me, hanging and writhing in body and soul.

"My God, my God, why hast thou forsaken me?"

I came to consciousness again. It must be dawn, for over in the direction of the clearing at the village I heard the cock crow three times. I had been betrayed. My wife had been betrayed. I gave up to die alone, without God. There was only me and my bloodied body swinging in the doorway. My last thought turned again to the Lord, "Don't let Hoa see me like this, please, God. Take me, but please do not let Hoa see me die like this."

✳ ✳ ✳

At 7:30 that same morning, wondering why Cam was so long in prayer and so late for breakfast, Hoa, having just finished her devotions, her heart ablaze with love for the Lord for his promises, cheerfully set out to take Cam his breakfast up at the church.

Fresno

February– December 1968

15
Losing Track

Saigon

Daddy got us out on the first flight. He never spoke of how he did it. I never asked, because he could do anything. There were thousands trying to leave: oil company executives, diplomats, rich Vietnamese, and Mother and I. It must have been God's will, because we got seats on the first plane. As we drove to the airport in near silence, the discussion stuck to a skeleton of details. "Go to Carolyn's, then decide." "You'll need to get a car." "Where will we live?" "Check with the bank at our San Bruno branch to verify our balance. I think we'll be okay."

We sat on hard benches at the airport, waiting. I saw a teacher from the Phoenix Study Group. She was leaving her class behind. Daddy was a little more at ease than he had been, his shoulders squared with resolve. He would not leave his call. The gospel needed to be preached. The sacrifice of this mission just kept going up. Straight up. Getting costlier and costlier, calling for greater and greater surrender. Daddy's commitment was up to the task. There were no tears save for the wetness in Mother's eyes. She was being obedient as well by going. Daddy was her life, and she was leaving him behind on the verge of death. I didn't know where I fit in.

We landed at San Francisco International Airport in San Bruno on a Sunday morning. Everyone was at church, so we took a taxi to Carolyn's apartment and convinced the landlord

159

that we were relatives recently evacuated from Vietnam. He let us in, and we collapsed in exhaustion in the living room, caught between dreams and nightmares and unearthly time zones. I was sound asleep on the couch when I awoke to a thin gasping scream. Without thinking, I rolled off the couch and under the coffee table, lying facedown with my hands over my head. Waiting for it. Then I heard Momoo crying and Mother's voice say, "Mom! Mom! We're home!" I breathed. This was San Bruno. Mills Street. I crawled out, embarrassed at being under that table at the reunion. Carolyn and Rich had dropped Momoo off at the house while they went to the store. They were going to be in for a surprise in a few minutes themselves. We called Conrad and Carmen and Roger in Fresno as soon as they got home from church. They hopped into their car and headed up the San Joaquin Valley. By that evening we were all together again. Except for Daddy.

We stayed with Carolyn and Rich for awhile, trying to figure out what to do. I was put back into my old bunk bed, which now belonged to my three-year-old niece, RaeLynn. It did not seem the same as it used to up on the top bunk, lying now above a three-year-old and seeing little plastic bunnies pasted on the wall beside me. This small three-bedroom apartment contained Carolyn and Rich, RaeLynn, Mother, Momoo, and me. Eventually the decision emerged that Mother and I would leave San Bruno and move to Fresno to stay with Carmen and her husband, Roger. Conrad was also living with them, so most of us, at least one parent and three quarters of the kids, would be under one roof. It also meant that Mother and I got the hide-a-bed in the TV room and continued the Saigon pattern of sleeping in the same bed.

The discussion lasted the entire spring and summer of 1968. How long would Daddy stay in Saigon without us? Where would I begin the ninth grade? What was going to happen? The family did not want to put me in school only to turn around and pull me out. There was no high school in

Saigon. Most kids of missionaries to Viet Nam went to Faith Academy in Manila or Morrison in Taiwan or Dalat in Malaysia. I wasn't going. Period. It would have been easier on my parents if I did. They could be together in Saigon, and I would be at boarding school. No. I was now dependent on sleeping with them, and the jump to boarding school was less possible now than when this whole thing started.

For the time being I was entered into Hawthorne Christian School in Fresno, a tough choice for Mother to make since it had Pentecostal connections. But with only a few months left for me in the eighth grade, she thought it best to spare me from reentering public school so far behind the other pupils. She spent her time writing to Daddy and looking for a house to buy so we would have someplace to return to when this was all over. On a little side street in Fresno, Sycamore Street, she and I walked in to look at a three-bedroom ranch and knew it was home. Her for the kitchen, and me for the pool. We immediately called Carolyn and Rich, and they agreed to move to Fresno and live in it while we were gone. The purchase of the house coincided with Carolyn and Rich's arrival at the end of the school year. I moved out of Mother's bed at Carmen's and back into the bunk bed above RaeLynn and spent the summer by myself in the pool. I grew so tan that Mother told Carmen she was almost embarrassed to be seen with me in public.

September rolled around without any definite leading from the Lord, so in an exchange of letters between Mother and Daddy it was agreed I would start the ninth grade at Tenaya Junior High School in Fresno. Starting the ninth grade was almost as frightening as the war. Mother took me down to register, and I was handed a sheet of paper listing the required supplies for gym. I had never been in a formal gym class before with showers and uniforms and towels and things. We went to Penney's and bought gym shorts and T-shirts and the smallest-size jock strap. This was a big problem because I had never seen one before. Once we got home, I hid in the bathroom and tried it on, the straps here, the straps there, until I figured it out. On the first day I walked to school with a brown grocery bag from Country Boy Market full of gym supplies. I carried it with me from class to class until fifth-period gym because I did not understand the idea of lockers even though I had a slip of paper in my pocket with an assigned locker number on it. When the bell rang, I went over to the big yellow building and found the door locked. I walked around to the back side, but the door had no outside handle. Desperately not wanting to be late, I hurried around the corner and saw a group of boys sitting in the field talking to an adult man in shorts. I walked up and entered the field through a gate. The man turned and looked at me.

"What's your name?" he snapped.

"Dan Peters," I said softly.

He looked down at his clipboard, running a finger down a long list of names. He finally said, "Okay, have a seat."

I sat at the edge of the group, and a couple of the big guys (they were all bigger than I was, but a couple of them were really big) started razzing me.

"Oooh, look at this kid, he brought all his stuff in a brown paper bag. What you got in there kid?" they asked and then burst into laughter, the joke totally lost on me.

"Aw, leave him alone," said one big blonde kid. Then he turned to me and said, "You new here?"

"Yeah."

"Where you from?" he asked.

I was stunned. I could not answer. I no longer knew. The question made my feet feel no longer attached to the earth, as though I simply floated. Oh sure, I walked here and there and rode my bike, but that gravity of the soul that keeps one attached to the earth was gone. I became conscious of myself in a way that made normal living impossible. It was as though I knew that I was adrift in the universe, that I had no power to determine my own direction or fate, that life was bigger than I was. Not only could I not control it, I could not even influence it. Too many nights I had sat in Saigon while the whole house rumbled with the guttural nausea of B–52 carpet bombings. Hanging onto the arms of the black lacquer chair, we had waited for it to cease but had no power to affect it in any way. I lived here, then there, slept in that bed or this one. No sense to it, no plan. I was no longer even a traveler, for travelers have a sense of where they come from and know where they are headed. I looked in at life from the place that only I knew. A private place, a lonely place.

San Bruno

If life was different for me now, it was most noticeable when I tried to reenter the Cedar Avenue gang. The whole gang came down to Fresno for my birthday in July. We walked around in our usual groupings and played ball and swam, and Michelle bought me a real baseball. Official. But there was a distance between me and them that I could not measure. They had changed as much as I had. The year and a half between leaving the seventh grade and starting the ninth produced mass changes in all of us, but we had also changed in different directions. They were doing things like adults, going places in cars, with an older sibling driving. Doing things like playing miniature golf. They invited me to join them once late that summer when Mother and I were visiting Aunt Esther and Uncle Johnny one weekend back in San Bruno. I had no idea of what to wear or how to act. Carmen's motherly instincts took over enough to get me some white jeans and a new shirt so that I looked almost normal. But looking normal was a long way from my sense of life. Ever since coming back I had been trying to participate in talk about baseball and girls and television, but it always seemed that while my words and theirs were derived from the same language, mine were empty of meaning, hollow. It was as though if you looked up my words in the dictionary there would be little blank spaces on that page. My body walked and talked and laughed, but there was a new distance between myself and it, and between myself and the people around me. This distance was new and sharp. I felt out of place when I first arrived in Saigon, yet I was still somehow present. But life back here, especially among all the kids at Cedar Avenue whom I knew and had grown up with, existed on the other side of a clear thin wall. I could see them through it. I could see myself acting on a stage while standing outside of it, unable to even push my hand through that clear thin wall. It was a mucousy substance of a wall that repelled me from even approaching it. Unfortunately, the night we went miniature golfing the bathrooms were on the other side of that wall.

Promptly at seven o'clock a car full of kids honked in front of Esther and Johnny's. I was sitting impatiently frozen on the couch tapping one foot when the honk made me jump with a rush of joy and fear. I approached the car, hoping to sit by Michelle to whom my heart still belonged. I was relegated to a corner of the back seat three bodies down from her, but that was close enough to see her kneecap, which sustained me all the way to the golf course in Redwood City. Never having been alone in a car full of kids, the driver being barely older than any one of us now, the loud babble of parental freedom seemed almost inappropriate. I could be loud myself, but in public we were supposed to be polite, and this seemed far from that. When we got out in the parking lot, the driver, who assumed authority for the evening, paired us up into two groups of four. She didn't put me in the group with Michelle but rather gave me her little sister Nan as my partner.

Through the wall I could see myself golfing and laughing. The only time the wall seemed gone was when I saw Michelle, but having no hope of her company, I slid back to my side of life. The windmills and the waterfalls that my blue ball skimmed around dominated my thoughts, until off in my consciousness I began to be aware that I had to go to the bathroom. It came on like a rush and stopped just short of the fatal point. I had no idea what to do. On my side of the wall there were no bathrooms and I could not find the power to go find one. There was nobody on my side of life to ask.

Saigon

We were the honored guests. Even though Pastor Loi had many children, I was the only child at the dinner table. There were Pastor and Mrs. Loi, Mother and Daddy, Trang and me. It was a feast of flavors that I still long for—sticky rice, nuc mum, spring rolls, black chicken chunks, and papaya. Mrs. Loi reached her short arms far into the middle of the table and snatched a goody with her chopsticks; then, looking at me with beaming black eyes, plopped it right onto my plate. I had seen those chopsticks glide in and over her lips all dinner long but now bowed my head and offered a thank you. Then, with a certain aplomb at being the center of attention, I balanced the prize to my own mouth and consumed her grace. Daddy winced.

Pastor Loi's house was down an alley in a dense Saigon suburb built for one-third the population it now held. Near the top of each wall a series of slots allowed the hot air to exchange with the hotter. Living far below our own riches in Phu's god-room, they fed us a lavish dinner to express honor to Daddy, who was their American boss. Many hands had inspected, washed, cut, stirred, and set this feast. But they were nowhere to be seen. After the formal introductions of his children were complete, they had all vanished into the house. Course after course ran through my plate, washed down by three glasses of tea. The tea hit suddenly.

Trang volunteered to show me to the bathroom. For some reason Mother and Daddy never had to go to the bathroom when it wasn't convenient. I *had* to go. I followed Trang down a long hallway, which dead-ended into the kitchen. It was still warm and filled with the smells of dinner. Through an opening in the wall we turned right into a large room lit by a dim bulb whose light did not quite reach the walls, leaving shadows to define its perimeter. Ah! Here were the Loi children, sitting on bags of rice and wooden stools. They all giggled when I came in. Trang lifted his skinny arm and pointed to the back wall.

"There," he said.

I walked over to the beginning of the shadow where he had pointed, only to discover a peeling plaster wall. Memories of the yellowed wall outside the PX flooded up in front of me.

"Here?" I quavered.

"Yes, there," he said.

There were girls in here! And they were all watching my every move. There was no choice. I *had* to go so bad this choice actually took little courage. I turned to the wall and reached for my belt buckle.

"No!" shouted Trang. "There!" he shrilled as laughter broke out throughout the room. He walked over to the wall and opened a door that I could have not distinguished had I tried all night long. I looked through the door to see the familiar Vietnamese-style toilet buried in the floor. I went in and shut the door. I did not want to miss and hit the floor but neither did I want to squat. I took a chance on missing.

Needless to say I was greatly relieved when I came out. I smiled at the cutest daughter on my way back even though she was now confident in her knowledge that Americans were about as dumb as humans can get.

San Bruno

By hole number five I was in trouble. I decided to wait it out until something happened, although I knew not what. I was paralyzed. I kept trying to play, desperate and in pain. The swollen feeling kept growing stronger until it slowly, inevitably began leaking out. I tightened and tightened but I could not hold everything. Gradually a small spot began to grow on my pants. I bumped into a set of rules I did not know and fears I could not avoid. At hole number seven the spot grew to the size of a silver dollar. Suddenly Nan threw down her golf club and said, "I have to go to the bathroom. Does anybody else have to go?"

My entire insides melted with relief. "I'll go with you," I said.

We walked up to the little hut, and she asked the man if there were bathrooms.

The manager looked up at us over a bucket of yellow and red golf balls and laughed, "Right around the corner, but only one of you in there at a time now, kids!" (He didn't know we were Christians.)

"Do you want to go first?" Nan asked.

"No, ladies first," I gestured.

Nan went in and after half a minute she came back out with a smile. "I'm done," she said. I went in, slammed the door, and practically flooded the place. Then reality struck. I was now fourteen years old, out with Michelle, and I had wet my pants. The green and white walls of that bathroom looked like a nice place to spend the rest of my life and I contemplated staying there. No one would notice; they would just go home, and life would go on, just as it always had. You could not stop it. Eventually, I flicked the little latch and stepped outside. Nan was waiting for me by the drinking fountain. We were quiet as we walked back to hole number seven.

After the game, with my pants not making any progress drying in the Bay Area's night air, I was assigned to sit by Michelle on the way home. In fact, it was so crowded that she had to sit on my leg. My dream come true, but I was so mortified that I sat with my head turned away and stared out the window. Would she notice? Was her skirt wet from my lap?

Both the me acting on the stage and the me on the other side of the wall rode home in silence.

Fresno

After we got back to Fresno we learned through the usual blue aeroform that Daddy had been assigned by the Pocket Testament League to Mexico City for a special evangelistic outreach at the 1968 Olympics. That meant he would be flying through Los Angeles on his way from Saigon to Mexico City and would be home for a few days. Above my protests Mother went by herself to pick him up at the airport. Thinking they would not be back till the next day, I rode my bike over to Triple J Drugs. Popping a wheelie into the parking lot, I suddenly saw a turquoise 1960 Buick Wildcat streamline past. Daddy's snow-capped head was a dead giveaway. I slammed on the brakes and left a strip of rubber on the sidewalk. Putting my head down and forward over the handlebars, I raced with the wind. My insides burst outward in energy, my legs pumped in a blur of speed, and my heart floated ahead calling for me to keep up. I turned off Seventh Street and saw the Buick in the driveway of the Sycamore house. I dumped the bike on the lawn and ran through the open door to find Carolyn and Mother laughing and crying and Daddy standing right in front of me. Having grown some, I almost knocked him over as I flung myself at him, shouting, whooping, and laughing.

Daddy may have regretted coming home because Carmen and Carolyn called a family meeting and convinced him not to leave me here in the ninth grade when he could take me to the Olympics, a once-in-a-lifetime opportunity.

"I will make up the work. I can do it" was my constant thesis.

For once in his life Daddy was ganged up on successfully.

That afternoon, surprisingly, Daddy bought me an expensive, real-leather, official NFL football at K-Mart. He had not seen me for nearly seven months since sending me and Mother home after Tet, and he wanted to do something special. Given his usual attitude about buying things, combined with how badly I had wanted this exact one, made this football a special treasure. After dinner we played a little catch in the front yard and as a result the football now sported its first good scuff. (I was going out for a pass, having made several great catches already and feeling pretty good about it, when a car turned the corner and I looked up to miss Daddy's wobbly but catchable throw. The ball landed in the street and scuffed.) But it was still an authentic football. A real football. A twelve-dollar football!

I might have been fourteen now, but there was not the slightest sign of maturity on my outward body, and my inwards were still part child and part adult, with little adolescence to be found anywhere in between. Today I had felt like a man, tossing the football with Daddy, but now, lying in the dark with my football in my arms, I started to feel an ache in my chest. I slowly started to cry, and I couldn't stop. By the light coming in from under the door I saw a shadow stop in the hall. Daddy had heard me crying. He opened the door and walked cautiously across the darkened, cluttered room. Kneeling down beside me, he said, "What's the matter, Pal?" Hearing the tenderness in his words and having him back from Vietnam broke my heart right open, and grief spilled everywhere. I swung my sleeve over my eyes and tried to wipe them dry and get control of my voice.

"I can't keep this football," I wavered. "I can't . . . it's wrong . . . it's wrong."

"Why, Pal?"

"This football costs twelve dollars and there are kids dying out there right now and twelve dollars would save them," I cried.

Images of little Vietnamese orphans digging through the garbage played on the wall above the bookcase. Their eyes were hollow, without hope. I knew that I might as well bomb those orphans as hold this football. The knowledge was not simply one of propositional truth but something I experienced as though it literally happened. If I kept this football, I would kill them. I lay there, clutching the bomb in my right arm, my left arm covering my crying eyes.

Daddy had no words. We had seen the war together, and he knew what I said was true. Finally, with the stale coffee breath that was a part of most of our conversations, he said, "Pal, God gives us good gifts sometimes, and it's okay to take them. He has given us this house when many people do not have houses. We didn't earn it; God gave it, and we should just be very thankful to him. I bought you this gift because I missed you so much the past few months and I wanted to give you something special. It's okay to keep it. The important thing is that we give our hearts to God so he can use us to help those kids when he calls us to do it."

Then, as usual, he prayed. And then, to end the embarrassment, I said I was okay. His explanation may have helped me go to sleep that night, but it did not diffuse the confusion—was this a bomb, or was it a special gift from Daddy and God? The confusion settled into a permanent discordant resonance and left me to walk an uneven, rutted road, first lurching to the left and then to the right.

Claremont 1995

16
Through Isaac's Eyes

Claremont, California 1995

I remember now one of the sermon illustrations Daddy preached back at Cedar Avenue Baptist Church before we left for Saigon. It was a foggy autumn Sunday morning on the peninsula. The dull bounce of light illuminated the inside of the church, giving it an even gray color, so that fog seemed to hang within as well. This sermon illustration sliced through the fog and pinned me motionless to the metal folding chair. I do not remember the sermon, only this story. It is about a missionary captured by the communists. I see it through Isaac's eyes:

A missionary to China and his boy were taken captive by the Communists during the revolution. The Communists threatened to kill the son unless the father denied his faith. He would not. So the soldiers laid the boy's hand upon the table and with a swift slash of forged steel they took off four finger tips. The boy screamed for his father.

The dull-eyed officer smiled and said, "Now you will deny this Jesus?"

"No" was the simple answer.

Once again the sword was raised and cut through flesh and bone sinking deep into the wooden table top. The sword squeaked in the bloodied splinters as the soldier rocked it back and forth to work it loose from the table top.

The boy fainted limp into the arms of the soldier pressing him to the table.

The communist officer raised his eyebrows at the missionary father.

"Oh God!" the missionary cried to the ceiling. His heart was being pulled apart ventricle from ventricle, the peritoneum, stretching white, toughly hung together, trying to keep the heart unrent. "No, I will not deny him" was the whispered answer.

The soldier shook the boy awake. He came to consciousness, screaming in pain, and terror darted through his eyes, searching for the father who held him when he cried, for the father who comforted him when he fell.

"Save me, Daddy! Save me!" the boy pleaded.

The father's knees buckled him to the floor, and he vomited in the dirt, whispering a guttural, "No ... Jesus. ... Please, Jesus. No."

The soldier again raised his sword and after a hesitation of eternity took the boy's hand at the wrist.

There was no denial. When they dug the graves, casting in first the body parts and then the dead bodies, there had been no denial of Jesus the Lord.

Whether the missionary died of a broken heart for his amputee son or by the sword himself is not known. The son died as the father's test of faith.

✳ ⸱ ✳

Just like all history, Daddy's life was divided into B.C. and A.D. His B.C. history was prehistory, little more than a background, the setting of the stage on which his real life would be played out. I know very little about Daddy's B.C. history. He himself seemed cut off from it—as though it was not an ongoing part of his life but rendered mute by a sharp cleavage of consciousness, of person. Yet there is a generational history, which must not be overlooked. Somewhere this generational line—its historical presence, its consciousness—came to culmination when Daddy took me to Vietnam.

Daddy's Daddy, Grandpa Johann, struck terror in Daddy's heart. I never knew Grandpa Johann because he died when Daddy was only ten. But Daddy had memories of him. Memories of riding the trolleys in New York City, playing catch in the house and breaking the vase on the mantle, walking hand in hand on Coney Island tempted by twirling cotton candy and fascinated by clanking gears on the Ferris wheel. The terror slicing Daddy's heart was not from the memories, not the thunder of the rod or the boom of the angry voice, but from the muffled, yet not too distant, screams. The screams of a voice raw in pain, shaking in consciousness just this side of shock. The screams choked by a dry tongue sticking to the roof of the mouth even as layer after layer of skin is slowly peeled back, singed from the fires of God's wrath upon the sinner. Christianity is very hard. Maybe liberals could get away with only a God of love—but we could not. We had to deal with reality. The reality that God's holiness is above his love and absolute in its demand. Daddy meant it when he begged from the pulpit, "Dear people, dear people...." In all his stiff-legged social demeanor, cool reserve, and stern doctrine, his heart broke open for the lost, for he heard the screams of Grandpa Johann, Daddy's Daddy.

Sometimes I pick up Grandpa Johann's pocket watch—the only connection from Grandpa Johann to Daddy to me. I grasp it in my fingers and can feel it in Daddy's hand, large and strong and firm, and sometimes, just at the edges, there is the hint of Grandpa Johann's hand. They are walking to the end of the pier and looking at the gentle Atlantic tide, Daddy's hand in his daddy's hand. Grandpa Johann takes the watch from his pocket with his left hand so as not to let go of Daddy's hand. He flips open the cover and it reads 8:00 p.m. It is time to go back to New Jersey and to Nina and George and little Madison. It is a good life. Three sons. America.

I do not hear the screams of Grandpa Johann from hell. I am afraid to listen. But I still hear the groans of Daddy in

prayer. Late on a Saturday night, alone on the church platform humbling himself before God, bearing the burdens of
his people, listening for the Spirit in the still. There I hear the
groans of Daddy. He knew what others did not. He understood the revelation of God—Jacob have I loved, Esau have I
hated. Oh the joy of being chosen, of being unworthy but of
being chosen. Oh the pain of knowing. Of knowing of the revelation of God's holiness.

God is seamless. A. W. Tozer describes God as the
absolute "absence of parts." Joy, Glory, Love, Mercy, Wrath,
Judgment—One. The sound of the judged cry in God's ears,
the same ears that ring with the shout of the praise of the righteous. One. Condensed into the human heart that Oneness
springs violently outward, to neighbor, to pulpit, to Vietnam.

Daddy was an orphan of sorts. His father was a successful shirt-pattern cutter, and later, an efficiency expert in New
York City. Working in the Jewish garment community, he
spoke Yiddish and built a good business reputation. Grandpa
Johann loved his work, his family, and his cigars. Born in Germany, married to an Englishwoman, he accomplished much,
but when confronted with the choice of quitting smoking and
continuing to live, or not quitting and dying, he died—the
cigar more important than his three sons. Shortly after his
death, his widow, Nina Peters, was stricken with tuberculosis
and was removed to a sanitarium to spend the rest of her days
there. The three boys were split up between relatives and
orphanages, and by the age of twelve Daddy was pretty much
supporting himself.

After high school he took to "riding the rails." He wandered up and down the east coast, in and out of New York,
Boston, and Philadelphia, his character sharpened to a finely
honed edge of independence, his heart tendered from the
pounding hammer of life. One night he slept in a haystack in
the country. He had walked quite a ways that day down a
lonely road and ended up, once more, nowhere in particular.

He awoke in the night with a start, his heart pounding, his skin sweating. Seeing a small service station on the other side of the road, he walked across the field to see what time the blue neon clock told. It was three-thirty. From a place within and below, he knew he must return home. Hopping the first train heading in the right direction, he arrived home two days later—just in time for his mother's funeral. The death certificate noted tuberculosis as the cause and three-thirty in the morning, two days earlier, as the time.

Two years later he paused in front of a chapel in New York City. The sounds of singing escaped through the open door and beckoned him in. Here he heard a story. God created the world. Humans rebelled and broke with God. They could never be good enough for God, who is perfect, so God made provision for their redemption by faith in Christ. His sins forgiven, Daddy's conversion was real and lifelong. He immediately did what the true convert did, he dedicated his life to full-time service to the King and went to Moody Bible Institute the following year.

He arrived at Moody in 1936. Here he entered a universe that was steeped in the traditions of D. L. Moody's evangelical revivalism and blazing with the heat of a particular form of spirituality emanating from England called Keswick. Here he would learn the content of the sermon and its effective delivery. Here he would find Ruby and, as evidence of the blessings of following the will of God, have his need for a family redeemed. It was here also that he learned the levels and layers of the human soul and how the Holy Spirit worked his way down through them all. All the way down to total commitment.

These were the "Stam years" at Moody. John and Betty Stam, Moody graduates of a few years before, had gone to China to serve God as missionaries. Hearing of the advance of outlaw bands upon their village, John Stam decided to stay and trust his sacred call to the village rather than heed the warnings and flee. The Stams were beheaded for Christ.

Their story was a compelling drama that permeated prayer meetings, revival sermons, Moody recruitment literature, and the hearts of Moody students: "Who? Who, my dear Christian friend, will God raise up to take their place?" The burden of their misjudgment was translated into the glory of martyrdom and was strapped not only to the back of their surviving infant, christened the "Miracle Baby" by the press, but to every student who traversed Moody's hallowed halls.

Fulfilling that destiny, Daddy applied to go to China as a faith missionary upon graduation in 1939. He was rejected because of bad health. Dejected, he did what he could: he became a "home" missionary, abandoning city life for a gospel mule. As newlyweds, he and Rube moved into the remote regions of the Ozarks to pastor a small, neglected congregation. Within a year too many lard sandwiches and lack of support drove him back to college and a conventional pastorate. But that still small voice calling for total commitment in missions was never silenced.

The Keswick spirituality, which guided the Stams and into which Daddy was baptized at Moody Bible Institute, was based on surrender—surrender of whatever it was that held one back from total commitment, even to the surrender of the person's own self, own personhood, own life. For unknown reasons, God requires sacrifice to satisfy his holiness. Abraham had to sacrifice Isaac to satisfy God, even though Isaac was delivered at the last minute by a bleating ram. God the Father completed this scenario by sacrificing his own innocent Son. Christians thereafter, while saved by the act of Christ, are asked to repeat this surrender to God and to follow Christ, to take up the cross and deny the self. To present their bodies a living sacrifice and to lay their all on the altar. Total commitment is simply not total unless it is tested by ultimate sacrifice, which for Daddy was not only his own self but, like Abraham, his willingness to sacrifice his family—the very thing that he treasured above all else, all else except the Lord. To test his total commitment, the Lord asked Daddy for his family. After his death I found this letter, which he had written to Mother two months after she and I were evacuated and he stayed behind in Saigon.

Saigon, April 2, 1968

7:15 p.m.

Dearly Beloved Rube,

     ... I remember shortly after I was saved, I made some decisions. A break once and for all with the former things. My heart and my mind have not always been faithful to those decisions which no doubt were of the Lord, but they have never been retracted, and never will be—only from time to time they must be it seems implemented with a new thrust of spiritual power and heart searching and self crucifixion. And regardless of where a person thinks or sees himself to be, there is always that voice in the backstage calling for a still greater dedication. A greater love. More of Christ and less of self.... I prayed about the Lord giving me a real peace of heart and mind if He wanted me to stay here—and face the constant bombing and mortar fire—and the Lord instantly answered it seems. And now if He wants me to stay here He will I'm sure give me the degree of spiritual power and victory for which I've groaned for weeks now that I don't have you to lean on and sort of cushion things for me. Now, alone, isolated it seems, half a world away from you, the conditions for the Lord's total takeover of every phase of my life has not only become desirable on my part, but absolutely necessary, and I feel that should it not be brought to its proper consummation that I shall die.... And during this time I'm praying for and expect, and am certain, that other problems, small and insignificant though they seem often to be, will find their solution in a total love for Christ and a crucifixion of self. The hardest thing in this world is to kill the self, and the Lord is the only one who shall succeed in that, but He is going to have the victory—and really already has it as far as I am concerned. . . . I am yours—totally—and His,

Johnny

Daddy had to go to Vietnam. He wasn't drafted, he was called. Called by an inner voice and a higher voice.

His inner voice beckoned him to the front lines. It needed the deafness of the artillery. It needed the adrenaline of facing the unknown and dark possibilities. It needed the manhood—Cambodia, Danang, the DMZ. Missing World War II as a minister with children, he had not yet faced up to it. He could not have made it in WW II anyway. The public showers, the burping in the mess tent, the farting in the barracks. He would have shown the aging of it like an old ceramic vase, tiny cracks running through the glaze. But now it was time. He had to do what he had to do, for himself. He did it. Ever after, he would say to me, "Pal, Vietnam was the pinnacle of my life, the best years of ministry I ever knew."

The higher voice called him to sacrifice his all on the altar for Christ. He understood what the average American Christian never could then and still cannot, when they sentimentally sing in church, "I surrender all, I surrender all. All to Thee, my blessed Savior, I surrender all." Most of them have no idea what following Jesus would truly mean if it meant *everything*. No, not your life in front of a firing squad, that's too easy. But your life on this earth and all that it holds—its possessions, its desires, its satisfactions, home, friends, family. Not to quickly die and be with Jesus—but to live without, in deprivation. Daily. The pain to bear the loss of all. "I surrender all," except the love of God. The stark hypocrisy of those who sing those words without thought still makes me upset to my stomach. They are profaning heavy and dangerous words. They may never swear, but their lips are profane. And the happy little notes that they send to Jesus swirl upward like the incense of dung and stink in his nostrils. God breathes them in, and he knows his people.

There on the front lines, his body on the line, Daddy was able to kill the self, the carnal self, and move to that spiritual state of being filled with the resurrected Christ where joy and sorrow mix and confuse the mind but clarify the vision of the heart.

I cannot see through Daddy's eyes, or through Mother's, the ironic self-fulfillment that came with self-sacrifice. I can only see through Isaac's eyes—for while he left the other three kids behind as adults, it was me, the favored heir, whom he tethered down on the altar of Saigon. An act that confused us both by the simultaneous joy of obedience and horror of human sacrifice.

Total surrender to God's will. In God's will is perfection. In God's will is security. In God's will is the knowledge that all things work together for good, even the sobs of little boys in the night longing for big brother, even ducking for cover as the shrapnel flies, even the decision to send Mother and me home, and for him to stay. God's will is that we present our bodies a living sacrifice. God's will is for the son to be sacrificed. This is the old, old story.

This ideology of sacrifice, of ultimate denial, of humans bearing the pain of the universe by the giving up of the self and the giving up of what one truly loves as the way to God, this is the Christian story. This story is rooted in the God/Jesus story, but does God condemn us to endlessly repeat it for our own salvation? And in sacrificing me, why is it that Daddy had the Epiphany of his life? This event bound me to him more deeply than any of the other kids were bound to him during his life. Bonded at the rib and the lung.

For me, the ram did not bleat. Why, after the barrel was packed, did the ram not bleat? Why not after resigning the pastorate, selling the house, or even boarding the plane? No bleat. Finally the knife plunged. With a cry to the heavens, a groan from a place within him below language, a groan that only the Holy Spirit could understand, with an act of courage, of faith, of knowing that without a bleat there would still be fulfillment of the promise and the ultimate eternal glory of God's will, with the love toward me of a father who would do only what is best and right, with the rending of his heart the knife fell. It pierced my skin, deflected off my rib and slid into my lung. I looked at Daddy, and he looked back as the lung slowly filled with fluids and blood. My life gathering at the river, crossing over. There was a mixture of joy and sorrow, grief and pain, centered in our eyes with the hope of tomorrow glimmering around the edge. Praise God. To this day I cannot breathe with clear lung or look into the memory of Daddy's eyes and not see orphaned boy, brave hero, tender father, holy saint, sacrificer.

Postscript

Fresno, California 1995

I sometimes now come to sit on the flat bottom of the San Joaquin Valley. On an earlier day, a clearer day, one could sit right here and look eastward up into the very face of the Sierras. The height, strength and stature of these white-headed mountains are now obscured by farm dust, crop spray, and too many tailpipes. Over to my left is an old stand of evergreens and tall cedars. It shades the old cemetery there, where a tall granite monument sits slightly askew, a straight and true testimony to the dead. But here, at Daddy's grave, all is flat, indistinguishable from the thousand flat lawns in front of the thousand flat houses of Fresno.

His smell of coffee, Vitalis hair cream, steam-ironed suits—and that particular odor of the work that he as a living organism emitted still lingers. Stale, pungent. The odor I have smelled on my own shirts after too long in the sun. Now he rots. Lying in an oak casket handmade by Austrian craftsmen, a gift bestowed upon him by some official whose job it was to choose caskets for foreigners who die in Austria, he rots. Crafted of golden oak with an angular top, it looked like sacred architecture. Under the soil of the San Joaquin, layers of slate and hardpan, Indian trails and dirt plowed by rusted tractors, here, lone, he lies.

How could such a life as Daddy's be contained here? The other graves nearby have flat marble stones with pictures, lilies, sparrows and verse. I can no longer look at the one two rows over that reads, "He looked like David, thought like Solomon, worked like Samson and he loved like Jesus." It is too true. But it rests on the grave of another hero.

Daddy's grave is unmarked except by a temporary chunk of concrete laid by the caretakers of the cemetery to identify the grave. It lies recessed in the grass encircled by a little dirt trench kept clean by a weed-eater. For Daddy there will be no tombstone. There will be no honoring the dead. There will be no dollar spent on the decaying bones of someone who is not really dead while people need the gospel. At his funeral the preacher said, "He left no estate, no fortune. He left a legacy of preaching the gospel. I need five men, today, to replace John Peters. Who among you will go?" None went. His influence had wasted away, overwashed by the gaseous egos of recent seminary graduates and deafened by the pleas of a hundred television evangelists. His day was gone. Knowing that the aged had no place in the American evangelical church, he had gone back to the field to die with his boots on. He did not tell us that an aneurysm already bulged thinly in his chest. No heart surgery for him, he was ready to go Home. He died in Austria, Wednesday night, after prayer meeting, on June 4, 1987.

Here I sit, knowing him and not knowing me. Perhaps I am him, and perhaps I am his very opposite. A relation that defines me, whispers to me . . .

"Be careful with those words, Pal. You can't ever take them back."

"I know, Daddy."

"Why don't you write about something worthwhile— Edwards, Whitefield, the apostle Paul . . ."

"You were the one who taught me to admire great men."

"You preaching yet, Pal?"

"All it takes is a call. If God calls, I'll preach."

"How's Rube?"

"She can't figure out why you dropped her off at Carm's and don't come to pick her up."

Silence.

"Daddy, when she dies, I am going to put a grave marker right here. I hope you don't bump your head on it at the Rapture, but it's going down right here. It's biblical, you know, to honor the father."

"Pal, why don't you write about something worthwhile."

"I will, Daddy, I will."